AMY BALLON (right) and DANIELLE BOTTERELL (left) are the co-founders of Admiral Road Designs and the mothers of five young children. Previously, Amy worked as a strategic management consultant, and Danielle spent five years in the investor relations and corporate communications field. Visit their website at admiralroad.com.

DR. REBECCA REUBER is a professor at the Rotman School of Management at the University of Toronto, where she teaches entrepreneurship to MBA students and executives.

PHOTO BY PAUL CHMIELOWIEC

MOM INC.

MOM INC.

How to raise your family and your business
without losing your mind or your shirt

AMY BALLON
& DANIELLE BOTTERELL

with Rebecca Reuber, Ph.D.

Collins

Published by Collins, an imprint of HarperCollins Publishers Ltd

First Edition

Mom Inc. is not published by or with the MOMpreneur® Networking Group Inc.
("MNGI"), the registered trademark owner in Canada of Mompreneur. The term
"mompreneur" is used in this book with the agreement of MNGI.

HarperCollins books may be purchased for educational, business,
or sales promotional use through our Special Markets Department.

HarperCollins Publishers Ltd
2 Bloor Street East, 20th Floor
Toronto, Ontario, Canada
M4W 1A8

www.harpercollins.ca

Library and Archives Canada Cataloguing in Publication
information is available upon request

ISBN 978-1-55468-626-1

Printed and bound in Canada
WEB 9 8 7 6 5 4 3 2 1

Mixed Sources
Product group from well-managed
forests, controlled sources and
recycled wood or fiber
www.fsc.org Cert no. SW-COC-002358
© 1996 Forest Stewardship Council
FSC
99%

In memory of Amy's mother, Jerry Ballon, and Danielle's grandmother, Yvonne Goldberg—mompreneurs ahead of their time.

And to our children, Jessie, Kyra, and Lily; and Charlie and Eve—may you follow your bliss.

Contents

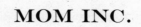

MOM INC.

In 2006, Canadian entrepreneur Sandra Wilson made international news when she sold her shoe company, Robeez, for $30 million. When she started her business in her basement twelve years earlier, she had no idea of the kind of success she would enjoy. On the contrary; back in 1994, Sandra was merely looking for flexibility in her life with a chance to still bring in an income. Her one-year-old son was in full-time daycare, and she was a laid-off airline worker. She wanted to be in control of her schedule and spend more time with her son.

Frustrated by shoes that wouldn't stay on her son's chubby feet, she cut up an old leather purse and designed her own. She made twenty-four pairs of booties and took them to the Vancouver Gift Show. Although sales in her first year were just $20,000, the response from buyers was positive and her business doubled in size each year.

Sandra was looking to be her own boss while being at home with her child. And just look at what happened when she did.

Introduction

What were we thinking?

If you're reading this book, it's likely because you're experiencing that uneasy feeling that many women before you have felt. It may have started creeping into your thoughts a little at a time, or it may have hit you like a ton of bricks. However you came to it, you're aware, and not in a good way, of the tension that exists between career and family. So, what to do?

If you had told us when we were in university that we would become entrepreneurs, we would have laughed out loud. (Frankly, if you had told us that we'd be buying Barbie dolls for our future daughters we would have laughed at that too.) No, we hadn't toughed it out for years downtown and then put ourselves through business school to pursue long days in a poorly heated basement—our visions were much more grandiose. We were going to meet each other for power lunches, in fabulous pantsuits, in between business trips. Over a glass of white wine we would whip out our leather Filofaxes (this was before BlackBerrys) to plan our next rendezvous. We were going to conquer the corporate world.

It didn't turn out that way. Business school was great. We learned lots, but more tangibly, we graduated with offers for our dream jobs in our pockets. Our starting salaries were ridiculously high. We would work at these corporate jobs, we thought, until we were ready to have children and then we would re-evaluate our careers. After giving birth we'd return to work part-time or find jobs that promised more reasonable hours.

What really happened was that we were forced to make these choices much sooner than we'd anticipated.

Graduating from business school in 2000 and 2001 respectively, Amy worked as a management consultant for a year before getting laid off; Danielle had her job offer rescinded as the economy tanked and never got the chance to start. The economic downturn that occurred as a result of the events of September 11, 2001, meant that we both found ourselves highly educated and seriously unemployed.

At the same time, Amy's mother, Jerry (an extraordinary woman and a heck of a mompreneur—beloved by us both), was in the midst of a terminal illness. Spending time with her in her final months forced us to prioritize what was really important to us in our personal lives. During this time we had a lot of opportunity to sit around and just think.

What could we do, we wondered, to put our degrees to use but avoid going back to corporate life? What would allow us to keep a foot in the business world while enabling us to be available for our families? We were thirty years old and both had babies on the brain. How on earth were we going to manage our high-powered careers while raising our children?

A mom we know told us that when working downtown she always felt like she left the office too early and got home too late. We too had the sinking feeling that no matter where we were, we'd feel like we should be in the other place. The bottom line? We wanted out of the rat race. But we still wanted to work, to learn, to be engaged in something beyond diapers and *Sesame Street*. We knew better than to buy into the myth of the Supermom. We've never believed that we could do everything at the same time. But we do believe that we have the power to choose which of the things we want most.

With this in mind, it was time to forge a new path. We didn't know it at the time, but we were about to become *mompreneurs*—that is, business owners who are juggling their work and their families at once. In 2002, we founded Admiral Road Designs, named for the street where our basement apartment "World Headquarters" was located. Since then, we've been shipping cozy, personalized fleece blankets to thousands of happy kids around the world. We've celebrated many successes and milestones, suffered many disappointments, and generally experienced the highs and lows of anyone who starts a business. At the same time, we've tried to balance the needs of our families with those of our company. We've learned a ton, met wonderful customers, suppliers, and employees, and generally had a terrific go of it so far, with the best yet to come, we hope.

(Before we continue, we want to state emphatically that we have nothing but admiration for the many bright, talented, creative, and most important, patient women who are full-time moms. We know and love many such moms and have often wondered on which side the grass is greener. All we know is that we aren't cut out for full-time, straight-up mommyhood. Same goes for the women who work outside the home full-time, whether because they must or because they just love it. This book is meant to dispel the myths and highlight the truths of mompreneurship without judgment on those who choose otherwise.)

The parallels between giving birth to a child and giving birth to a business are not insignificant. In this book, we will take you through the process of what's involved in planning, conceiving, and raising your business—all in the context of motherhood. We want to provide a practical framework in which to consider the question, "Is mompreneurship for me?" We will suggest ways to generate and evaluate your ideas. We'll then take you through the process of how to plan and eventually run your business.

And drawing on the experiences of other mompreneurs, we'll talk about what it's like to be engaged in starting your own company with a baby stuck to your boob. Or in a meeting with a Cheerio stuck to your butt (we have actual experience with this one). We'll address what you truly need to consider when juggling the competing demands of a growing child and a growing business. We'll also let you in on what mompreneurs know about being truly successful. It is our hope that you'll refer back to sections in this book that are relevant to you as you experience them with your own venture.

We believe that mompreneurship is about accepting trade-offs, making choices, and focusing on the things that matter to you most. We hope this book will help you determine what those things are—it's one of the main reasons we wanted to write it.

We want to share with you tales from the trenches. We're not talking about lessons we learned in business school. (We learned a lot there, but an MBA is by no means a prerequisite to having a successful business.) The experiences we've had as mompreneurs have made us laugh, cry, and cringe in disbelief. We've enjoyed the camaraderie of other women and have been backstabbed by the "sisterhood." We've seen ideas that range from the innovative to the inane. We've witnessed plenty of start-up successes and failures (our own and others).

When we began to think about this book, we had a good base of knowledge from our own experiences as well as those of our mompreneur friends. But we wanted to paint as broad a picture as possible. So we sat down and had conversations with more than fifty mompreneurs. We talked to women in multi-million-dollar businesses, and women who are struggling to make ends meet. We met women whose businesses blew up and women who have opened up and conquered whole new categories. We met with partners, sole proprietors, single moms, gay moms, and moms of children with special needs. We talked to mompreneurs about their marriages, their bank accounts, and the state of their health. They told us about the difficulties of juggling children and business, their pride and sense of accomplishment, and the many ways that they define success. They shared not only their war stories, but also their advice and tips for the mompreneurs who come after them.

Just to make sure we had the whole story, we also surveyed another two-hundred-plus mompreneurs. These busy and generous women shared their stories, observations, and advice. All in all, we collected volumes of information. Interestingly, as different as the women we chatted with and surveyed are, a good number of universal themes cropped up. Certain observations and conclusions were made by nearly every woman we talked to. And every mompreneur had something interesting and unique to add to the discussion—all of which we wish someone had told us before we started our business. So we'd like to share what these amazing women had to say with you. (You may notice that in some cases we don't provide the name of the mompreneur who provided a certain insight. Basically, we want to protect the privacy of the mompreneurs who shared with us, and we certainly aren't in the business of making anyone feel uncomfortable. Ultimately, we believe that what is said is more important than who says it.)

We've never claimed to be experts in small business. We are experts only in our own experience. That's why we called in the pro. Becky Reuber, Ph.D., is a researcher, professor, and consultant in the area of entrepreneurship at the Joseph L. Rotman School of Management, University of Toronto. She virtually wrote the book on entrepreneurship and she will lend her voice to this one. Becky is also our teacher, mentor, and friend. As the mother of three girls, Becky knows a thing or two about juggling her career with motherhood too.

There are many books out there that will tell you how to start your own business. We didn't set out to write the definitive guide on that topic—rather, we want to offer advice and tips from the women who have already gone down the path. And, while much has been written about mompreneurs, we've often noticed that the stories about mompreneurship are a little one-sided. There are accounts of fabulously successful companies run by happy moms who have lots of time to raise their children. It looks—well—perfect. Not much has been written, it seems to us, about *what it's like* to be a business owner and a mother at the same time. We wanted to let women who are considering mompreneurship know that while there is much to be said for forging your own path, it's not perfect. What is? Like anything, there are pros and cons.

We hope this book will give you a sense of life as a mompreneur while providing you with practical advice and helpful strategies for growing your business and your family at the same time.

We've been on the mompreneur ride for a while now—and it can be a wild one. We encourage you to jump on the roller coaster and join us. We invite you into our world for a candid and brutally honest look at mompreneurship. We want to share with you the good, the bad, and the sticky.

Top secrets about mompreneurship (or things we wish someone had told us)

1. Bringing your business to life is exhilarating
2. Mommy guilt and mompreneurship are a brutal combination
3. Your notion of success will be redefined (and that's a good thing)
4. Working on your own can be lonely
5. There is an awesome community of mompreneurs out there
6. Balance and flexibility are hugely rewarding
7. You're never more popular with your kids than when your work phone rings
8. It's hard to strike it rich
9. If you do what you love you're more likely to succeed
10. Not having to ask permission to go to the dentist rocks!

PART 1

PLANNING:
SHOULD YOU BECOME A MOMPRENEUR?

*Much as you'd (ideally) plan for parenthood, you'll need to plan
for mompreneurship. Here we'll look at the questions you'll need
to ask yourself before deciding whether juggling your own
business and motherhood is for you.*

1

Is mompreneurship for you?

The answer to your prayers?

Let's step back and define what a mompreneur is. (People also call us mom-entrepreneurs, momtrepreneurs, entrepreneurial moms, etc.) In our opinion, a mompreneur is any woman who has started her business with a view to having some availability or flexibility to be with her children. First, we don't get hung up on whether women start their business before or after having children. We, rather atypically, started ours in anticipation of family demands. Most women come to mompreneurship once the children are in the picture, but tomato, to-mah-to, we say.

Second, we have noticed that many mompreneurs start baby-focused businesses. It makes perfect sense—we all know how all-consuming a new baby can be, so what could be more obvious than starting a company to meet some demand in the baby marketplace? (In our case, it also occurred to us that if we were about to have children, so was nearly everyone else we knew, and we'd have a built-in customer base to start with.) However, a baby or kid-related business does not a mompreneur make—any business qualifies.

Third, we distinguish between mompreneurs—women attempting to balance family and career—and female Big "E" Entrepreneurs—who may be working a hundred hours a week and aren't with their children during the workday. This may be contentious, and we certainly don't want to imply that we think that female Big "E" Entrepreneurs are anything but total rock stars. We are not suggesting that mompreneurs don't sometimes work insane hours or juggle children and work, or that female Big "E" Entrepreneurs who work the big hours aren't available, loving mothers. We simply believe that a mompreneur is defined by at least a little bit of "mom time" in the workweek.

While we're in potentially contentious territory, we should point out that starting a business in order to have flexibility to be with children is for many women a luxury. For many, mompreneurship is a choice about balance and lifestyle, and not just about money. We'll tell you about a few women who went out and started businesses because they had no other means of paying the bills, or who started their businesses part-time while working full-time, as well as mompreneurs who are the primary earners in their homes. However, we'd be remiss if we didn't note that many mompreneurs are not immediately counting on the income. Someone, usually her spouse, is able and willing to keep the family afloat in the early days of the venture.

When talking to people about what a mompreneur is, something interesting comes up. A few of the women we spoke to bristled at the term. During one conversation a woman pointed out, "I'm not in this because I'm a mom. It works well that I'm a mom. I want to be recognized in my own right." Another woman says, "I don't identify myself as a mompreneur but as an entrepreneur who is also a mom. I feel there is a difference." Some women are downright irked by the term. We recently came across a (female) Twitter user who vowed to "unfollow" anyone who uses the word mompreneur in her profile.

This backlash is a stark contrast to the way the two of us articulated our roles when we started our business. Having just come from the corporate world, we knew we did not want to work the crazy hours of a straight-up Big "E" Entrepreneur. We always made the distinction that we were entrepreneurs who wanted to work part-time so we could be available to our kids, even before we'd heard the term mompreneur. But that doesn't mean we haven't taken our company very seriously or that it's not successful. It also doesn't mean that we don't get our backs up when someone (usually from business school) asks us if we are "still doing our little business." After all, it's not a puppy dog or a fuzzy rabbit—it's an honest-to-goodness revenue-generating, tax-paying organization, with everything that entails.

We wonder if it's a matter of perception. Perhaps for some the term mompreneur conjures images of a woman selling a few hair barrettes at a local school craft sale. Not so, or more accurately, maybe not so. The types and sizes of mompreneur businesses are as varied as the women themselves. We spoke to women with very small businesses, just bringing in a few dollars or even just keeping themselves engaged while home with kids, and we spoke to women with multi-million-dollar businesses. A mompreneur runs her own business while making time in the workweek to be with her kids. Period. Mompreneur is not a bad word or a demeaning term. And while we're at it, why do we need to look down on the mom selling the hair barrettes, anyway? This is a woman who creates, markets, and sells something. We say, "Good for her." Looking down on each other and judging each others' efforts is the kind of thinking that sends us right back to the dark ages. The truth is that the only way for anyone to truly control their schedule is to own their own business. We applaud anyone who starts any size business for any reason—it's a heck of an effort.

Why mix business with motherhood?

There are millions of female entrepreneurs in North America, many of whom are, of course, mothers. Statistics looking directly at mompreneurs are limited, but we do know that it is a rapidly growing trend. According to a 2006 study by CIBC, there has been a dazzling fifty percent growth in the past fifteen years in the number of Canadian women who are self-employed. What's more, the number of women entrepreneurs is rising sixty percent faster than the rate of men entrepreneurs.

News out of the United States also indicates a major uptick in the number of women entrepreneurs. According to the Center for Women's Business Research, the number of women-owned businesses in the United States grew at twice the rate of all firms between 1997 and 2002. And women with children are jumping in—each with a different business goal, a different family situation, and a different strategy to balance it all.

Mumpreneurship is also a huge trend in the United Kingdom. British Telecommunications plc conducted a 2009 study on the subject. The study found that ten percent of moms surveyed were planning to launch their own businesses because of a growing desire to have more flexibility in their working lives. Choosing the hours they work, achieving a better balance between their work and family life, and being their own boss were the top three most-cited reasons.

Our observation is that there is a correlation between paid maternity leave and the appetite moms have to start their own businesses. Where we live, the federal government extended employment benefits in 2000 to provide a full year of maternity leave. In our opinion, mompreneurship has exploded onto the scene as a real option for women since that time. Many women realize in that year that they don't need or don't want to return to their previous career, or at least not to the job they were in. It makes sense: becoming a mother is a huge transformation. We fall madly in love with our babies. And after spending a year at home, the thought of leaving him or her to return to work can be heartbreaking. Worse, the costs of childcare can make the return to work less than attractive.

So what are the reasons women are opting to become mompreneurs? They are as varied as the women who take it on. We didn't want to work the gruelling hours of our corporate pasts (little did we know!). Our three-point plan was to (1) have a project to keep us engaged while at home with our young kids, (2) earn enough money to supplement our family income, and (3) grow a business to the point that it would be ready to take off at the same time as our children were.

We've already talked about how we see the difference between a mompreneur and a Big "E" Entrepreneur, but in essence we wanted to respect the fact that the goals we set and measured for our business were commensurate with the time we had to devote to them. But we're just two of the millions of mompreneurs out there.

KNOW THY MOTIVES!

We can't stress enough the importance of knowing what you're looking for in embarking on mompreneurship. We suggest making a list of your top few goals—for example, be available to kids, earn $40,000 a year, etc. Keep your list somewhere you can see it. You will come back to this list more often than you can imagine. Mompreneurship isn't necessarily a get-rich-quick scheme and it may take longer than you anticipate to meet all your goals— it's essential to remind yourself why you went down this path.

Let's take a look at some of the top reasons women with kids take on a business. Odds are good that more than one of these reasons, plus your own unique ones, will apply to you.

I can't bear to leave the kids, and we need the cash

For some women, being available to their children is a long-standing dream. These mompreneurs tend to start their businesses so that they can afford to be home with the kids, more than for any other reason. Jennifer Torres is a mom to two girls and the founder of Salsa Babies, a program offering dance classes to moms with babes in arms. A former administrative assistant, Jennifer tells us, "I always knew I wanted to stay at home with my kids—long before I had them. I think it even affected my career choices prior to becoming a mom. On my maternity leave I was desperately trying to come up with an idea that would allow me to work from home."

For other women, wanting to be at home is something that comes upon them more gradually. Anita MacCallum, mom to two daughters, ages six and nine, left her job at an accounting firm to strike out on her own as a bookkeeper. Anita says, "I was five months into my six-month maternity leave and I knew I couldn't go back. I was so pained at the idea of being separated from my baby that I thought, 'This has got to work out some way.' I've been opposed to having strangers look after my babies—that was the worst thought for me."

We bet a few moms reading this can relate to that desperate, painful dread of separation.

It may be the case that the income from your job doesn't cover childcare costs. Perhaps your spouse's career is incredibly demanding and for logistical reasons one parent needs to be home. The particular stories are limitless, but the desire to be home with their children definitely leads many women to mompreneurship.

I want to be home with the kids, but my brain needs more

Maybe you've already made the decision and the necessary financial arrangements to be home with the kids, but you somehow feel that you need to be engaged in something besides motherhood. Elizabeth Kaiden opened up Two Rooms, a workspace with childcare for self-employed parents in New York City. We love how she explains her need for something more.

"If you take a job, in some sectors, in New York, you are expected to work sixty hours a week," Elizabeth says. "If you have a family, that's crap. I didn't want to do it. But I was also uncomfortable with the notion of being at home full-time. I didn't want to accept it. I was anxious about losing my sense of self, my ability to think, my earning capacity. I thought I would drift. I was afraid. I wanted to be home with my kids, but not exclusively. I wanted something that kept me in the world, that made me feel like a grown-up."

We think many women can relate to this sentiment. In fact, one mompreneur we know suggested that mompreneurship is a great place to hide. In other words, some of us mompreneurs are wary of *just* being stay-at-home moms, and having our own business lends a legitimacy to our daily lives that otherwise wouldn't exist. We've spent quite a bit of time wondering about that equation. Why is it that there is somehow shame or a feeling of wastefulness for some women at the notion of "only" being a mother? But that may be a subject for a whole different book. The fact remains that this sense of needing to be seen as more than a mom exists for many, and mompreneurship can give some women a sense of purpose beyond motherhood. For women who are fortunate enough to be able to afford to be home full-time, having a business can be a great place to stretch the intellect and stay connected to the world, while at the same time taking at least a mental break from the marathon of motherhood.

I love what I do, but I need to lose the nine-to-five thing

Those moms who are lucky enough to have found their true calling and have firmly established themselves in their careers may be ambivalent about the choice between office and child-rearing. After all, if you've just spent the past ten years climbing the ladder, growing professionally, and becoming known in your field, walking away can be distressing to say the least. At the same time, however, the hours and schedules of corporate life do not always mesh with motherhood, as we well know. So what's a mom to do?

For some of the mompreneurs we spoke to, it was a matter of reinventing their careers. In an age of conservation, these women have recycled their former careers into something that works for them.

Naomi Kriss is the founder of Kriss Communications. Her niche firm specializes in communications strategies for designers and architects. Before she had children, Naomi was the communications manager for a prominent (and male-dominated) architecture firm. Her hours were long, she worked extremely hard, and she developed a great reputation in the architectural community. After having her first child, she surprised her employer by choosing to return to work. Maternity leave was typically a woman's graceful exit from the firm. However, she insisted that her hours not be so crazy, and she found strategies to work better, smarter, and faster. When she got pregnant again, she knew that she had hit the end of her corporate road. On her second maternity leave, she decided to spend the first six months just hanging out with her baby and the second six months developing her business plan. She knew exactly what she wanted to do and, before her leave was up, told her firm she wasn't returning.

Naomi says, "I needed more of a balance between my work life and my personal life. Inside I was screaming, 'I can do more!' I loved the idea of building a business and worked hard to figure out how to continue doing what I love while also having time for myself and my family." Today Naomi has three boys, ages nineteen months to seven years, and continues to be a sought-after marketing professional who is in control of her own schedule.

If you've got a marketable skill set, you might just be able to retrofit your old career into your new life.

Or perhaps you'll find an entirely new gig that will still afford you a more flexible schedule. Elisa Palter and her business partner, founders of the successful *Help! We've Got Kids* directory books and website, met through volunteer work. They were both working in jobs with "crappy" hours. They weren't ready to not work, but they were moms who wanted to be there for their kids. Also, as MBAs, they had already made the commitment to being business people. They came to their idea together and decided they would work while the kids were in school from "carpool-to-carpool." Elisa and her partner recently sold their business after sixteen happy and successful years carpool-to-carpool, and are moving on to new ventures.

I need to pay my bills!
....

Either by necessity or by choice, some mompreneurs are born out of the need or desire for money. None of the mompreneurs we talked to shared a more dramatic story than Andrea Page, creator of FitMom. FitMom is an international company that provides pre- and post-natal fitness instruction. On her own since the age of fifteen, Andrea became pregnant at the age of twenty-six. Single and as yet not established in her career, she was in a very difficult situation. Her doctor told her not to exercise while pregnant. As a former personal trainer and gymnast, this was devastating (and unnecessary in her case) advice. Not only did she gain sixty pounds during her pregnancy, but she became depressed, bordering on sui-cidal, according to Andrea. After her son was born, Andrea was forced to go on welfare. "I couldn't even afford diapers. FitMom was born of desperation. I needed to create options for myself in an area in which I had experience," says Andrea.

Here's an interesting example of working for the money. Jan Frolic, owner of Magazine Network, a very successful media com-pany, has found her business to be a case of "golden handcuffs." She bought the company she worked at before she turned thirty and grew it rapidly on her own. Once her kids came along, she "learned to hate" her business. "I'm a natural-born stay-at-home mother. I wanted to be with my kids, not at the office," says Jan. The most logical plan for their family was for Jan to run Magazine Network while her husband stayed home with the kids in the early years. As the primary earner, Jan simply couldn't afford not to be working in her business. Jan feels different from a lot of mompreneurs, "I didn't start this with $10,000 and a dream," says Jan. Rather, she gambled big up-front with the purchase of the business, and stayed in it mainly for the money. Jan continues to work hard at finding harmony between working and raising her three kids but feels that she is finally successfully achieving better balance.

Ask anyone who has started a business—it's definitely a lot of work. You'll hear us say often that all motivations for self-employment are valid. But believe us, getting into it for the cash is a great reason.

I want to fulfill a dream

But what if it's not about the money? There are mompreneurs out there who took the opportunity to follow their bliss and fulfill a long-standing dream. Devorah Miller, the clothing designer behind Red Thread Design, says that she has "always needed to make things." She started sewing clothing for her three daughters and her creativity was stimulated even further. For Devorah, the choice to start a business was not about achieving balance. She was actually very happy in the job she was in. Rather, a self-described "fabric-aholic," Devorah took advantage of the career break that maternity leaves provided her to start her clothing business.

Alison Kramer, mom of three, turned her staunch support of breastfeeding into a business with the creation of Nummies, which manufactures stylish and functional nursing bras. According to Alison, "I was very passionate about breastfeeding, moms, and babies.

I'm very motivated by my feeling of the importance of breastfeeding. It's a small thing, but if a woman feels like she looks good while nursing she may want to breastfeed longer."

Erica Ehm, one of Canada's first veejays, was an after-school hero for chicks of our generation. (If you don't remember tuning into MuchMusic and watching Erica and JD Roberts as a teen, then you either lived in a very remote community or you're quite a bit younger than we are!) She still rocks as the force behind the Yummy Mummy Club, an online community for moms across the country. Erica says, "When I was an on-air personality, I was totally passionate about music. My job was a daily turn-on. When I had children, I wanted to turn my passion for my family into a career. Like in my former career, I have remained a communicator. Now I just have a different audience."

Whatever your passion or dream, turning it into your new job can make a lot of sense. Goodness knows you'll be up to your eyeballs in it in no time. You may as well be up to your eyeballs in something you enjoy.

I've got a nagging idea that just won't quit

For scores of mompreneurs, a great idea motivates their decision to enter the business world. Of the more than two hundred and fifty women who provided material for this book, more than sixty percent told us that they started their business for this reason. A great idea can come from many sources.

Tricia Mumby is one of the four moms who founded Mabel's Labels—a company that makes personalized labels. Tricia tells us that before they started their own business, each of the four partners was working in a job they thought they'd retire in. Julie Cole, her soon-to-be partner, had four kids in daycare who kept losing all of their things. She needed some help keeping better track of blankets, bottles, shoes, etc. Julie repeatedly asked Tricia when she was going to put her printing expertise to work and make her some labels. The idea wouldn't go away, and eventually Julie, Tricia, and their partners (and relatives) Julie Ellis and Cynthia Esp got together and began what is now a sizeable and successful business.

Or maybe you're already doing something terrific and you identify a business opportunity within it. Jordan Maher was new to her city when her first child was born. She explored museums, galleries, and different neighbourhoods with her baby in tow. Soon members of her moms group wanted to join her. It occurred to Jordan that there was a demand for organized tours for moms and babies, and that she was the woman for the job. She opened her first business, Moms in the City, not long after.

SOMETHING ON YOUR MIND? HOW TO KNOW IF YOU SHOULD PURSUE YOUR BUSINESS IDEA

If an idea keeps you up at night for three months, then you should do it.

—Nicole Morell, Honey-bunch.com

If you're worried that someone else is going to beat you to it, then it's probably a good idea.

—Sarah Morgenstern and Minnow Hamilton, SavvyMom.ca

I always wanted to be an entrepreneur when I grew up

Some people are just born entrepreneurs. Maybe you've always known that you have your own business in you.

Jacqui Meiers, a mom who owns GoneShopping.ca, an online retail store, has a dramatic story about her path to mompreneurship: "I was hospitalized with a near-fatal condition. When I was lying there, thinking about what I would have liked to have done in my life, two things came to mind: (1) I wanted to see a Madonna concert and (2) I wanted to have done something entrepreneurial." She adds, "I've worked in finance my entire career. And a corporate job pays enough to kill the entrepreneur in you." Jacqui started her business not long after and continues to run it part-time while maintaining her full-time career. (As soon as she recovered, Madge came through town and Jacqui rocked out at her concert.)

What the overwhelming majority of not-yet mompreneurs we've met have said to us is this: "I haven't come up with *the idea* yet, but I don't want to go back to work. I want to replace my income while being at home with my kids."

As you can see, there are tons of reasons why women consider mompreneurship. But the question is, should they take the leap? More importantly, should you? We believe that the bottom line is this: your reasons for taking the plunge are your own—whether you want to fulfill a lifelong dream, or just be engaged while home with the kids, or be the next Fortune 500 CEO. You will come back to your initial reasons time and time again, so it's important to be clear on them. Your experience with mompreneurship only has to work for you.

We've just told you about lots of women who successfully articulated their motivation for mompreneurship and launched their ideas. Believe us, if you take no other advice from us, take this: know *why* you're getting into this. There is no way you'll know *what* you're getting into. We'll do our best to shed some light on it, but it's a bit like childbirth—you can't truly appreciate it until you've been in the stirrups. No matter what, it's not going to get easier from here. Hang on . . .

2

Timing is everything

When to make the leap

So you're sold. The question now is not whether you want to make the leap into mompreneurship, but whether the timing is right for you. Let's take a look at the chronological points of entry into mompreneurship.

Before you're knocked up

We started Admiral Road before becoming moms. We had nearly a full year in business before the first of our collective five children was born. Many mompreneurs get their companies off the ground before they have kids. We chose entrepreneurship because we wanted to control our schedules. But many mompreneurs who birth their businesses before their kids were always going to be entrepreneurs no matter what. After they become parents they rejig their businesses to mesh with parenthood. In some cases this is an easy transition, but certainly not always. On the upside, starting your company before your family allows you the one thing you'll never get back—guilt-free time to work hard on it. Your spouse may not be thrilled by your disappearance for days or months on end in the early days of your business, but we all know that husband guilt has nothing on mommy guilt!

Getting your business up and running before your kids can be a great luxury and is undoubtedly easier than the alternative. Look at Debra Goldblatt, the PR maven behind rock-it promotions. Her über-successful firm had been running for years before she had her first child. With her business established, she can now better appreciate the time with her little one. And Trish Magwood tells us that she can't imagine how she would have grown her cooking school (and subsequent TV show and cookbook) business without the four years she spent "with her head down" before having her first child.

On the downside, the changes in your life that a new baby brings can be even more explosive in your business. Here's a bit of bad news: depending on where you live, there may not be maternity benefits available to you as a sole proprietor. But money is only one factor to consider. Nothing in your business will stop when your water breaks. Your customers, suppliers, and staff will still need things from you. So, even if you have maternity benefits or have stashed enough cash away to be able to slow down for a few months, the momentum of your business can make slowing down difficult.

We're huge fans of mompreneur extraordinaire and mother of eight, Victoria Sopik. She is a born entrepreneur who, with her business partner, runs Kids & Company, a national childcare chain. Sounds pretty good, right? Well yes, and no. As Victoria tells us, "I was signing paycheques ten minutes after I had my third child. For every single one of my children, I was off work the day they were born, and that's it." We'll talk about ways to mitigate the maternity-leave issue (we think this is one of the best arguments in favour of mompreneur partnerships), but we can tell you that our "mat leaves" spanned from a couple of months down to forty-five minutes. And, assuming you can deal with the mat-leave situation, there is the matter of your reduced intelligence, intermittent personal hygiene, and general concentration. Try figuring out how to use a can opener on two hours of sleep—and then think about getting on a call with a key client!

Finally, and we truly hope this doesn't happen to you, sometimes starting a business in anticipation of children doesn't work out the way you intended. Eryn Green of Sweetpea Baby Food and Organic Snacks knows this only too well. She and her business partner Tamar Wagman started Sweetpea when Tamar's first child was a newborn. They had a plan for growing their families as well as their business. But when the time came for Eryn to start her family, things didn't go according to plan. Ask anyone who has experienced difficulty getting pregnant and they'll tell you, it's hell. Then imagine having to go to baby shows and events (where there are literally thousands of pregnant women) on a regular basis while living through it. Eryn and Tamar found a way to make it work for them, and we're delighted to report that Eryn just gave birth to a beautiful baby girl, but the ride was certainly rough for Eryn. Like we said, we wouldn't wish that kind of struggle on anyone, but we do ask you to keep the remote possibility in mind.

While there's a bun in the oven

What better place to put all of those organizational nesting hormones to use than in your own business? We spoke to only a handful of women who did it this way and, boy, do we take our hats off to those who did. Take Julie Kenney, owner of Jewels and Pinstripes and celebrity gifting expert. She started her business while on bed rest. She certainly had time to make the calls she needed to convince organizers of a high-profile event to take her on for celebrity gift bags. As Julie tells it, "I had no logo, or even a company name! I just had an idea that I could do it." Today Julie runs what we think is the best celebrity gifting company around.

If you've got a mind to start your own business, then during pregnancy may be the time for you, morning sickness permitting. After all, take it from us: kids are a lot easier to take care of when they're still on the inside, no matter what your pregnancy offers up. Just keep in mind that you'll be at least temporarily sidelined after the arrival of your bundle.

During maternity leave

If you're lucky enough to live where we do and are gainfully employed, then giving birth means a full year of government benefits. But no matter where you live you're likely to have some dedicated time to be at home with baby. This period is for many women the time to make the leap into mompreneurship. After the first little while you've probably gotten into the swing of things, or at least learned to survive on no sleep and appalling nutrition. And odds are good it has at least occurred to you that you could get used to this motherhood gig. Besides all of that, you're actually receiving a monthly cheque (and if you're thinking about self-employment, it could be a while before you see a paycheque again!). So is it the perfect time to take the plunge?

FROM THE MOUTHS OF MOMS
During maternity leave might not be an ideal time to start a business. You're sleep-deprived, your hormones are out of whack, and you may not be thinking straight.

—Nicole Morell, Honey-bunch.com

Samantha Linton, mother of three boys and owner of Cleopatra Productions, became a mompreneur when she decided to make an erotica video for women. (Let us tell you, *that* was a fun interview! When Samantha debuted her video at an adult entertainment trade show in Las Vegas, her booth was sandwiched between the Valhalla Swingers Club and Bubba's House of Ass.) She had been developing the idea for several years beforehand but capitalized on the break from the workplace to get it off the ground. Samantha explains, "I know that some people regard mat leave as a very hectic time. For me, my third maternity leave was a huge break from my job. The baby really did sleep for the first three months and I took advantage of that opportunity to focus on my new business."

Lisa Will of Stonz, which makes boots and other cold weather accessories for little ones, took this approach: "I started on my mat leave. Then I returned to work. As an electricity trader I worked from 5:30 a.m. to 2:30 p.m. Then I'd come home, cut fabric on my kitchen table, and run around to sewers for a few hours before picking up my son. When my daughter was born, I was able to grow the business more while on maternity leave again."

You may have heard that it takes a few years to get a business up and running. We assure you that we'll be coming back to this point, so read on. Since it's unlikely that you will grow your business to the point where it pays enough for you to quit your day job, you may need to return to work after the maternity leave is up.

When you're working full-time

And then there are the mompreneurs who start their businesses part-time while working full-time. The biggest perk of this strategy is obviously the steady income stream and job security from your day job. And, you can get all of your ducks in a row before you officially open for business. You can take your time planning and hang out your shingle when the timing is perfect for you. This approach requires a lot of energy and discipline. Try to imagine getting yourself and your kids up and out the door, working a full day, bringing the kids home for dinner, bath, and bed, and *then* sitting down to work. Sounds exhausting, doesn't it? On the other hand, it's also excellent training for real life as a mompreneur. The other downside is that it may take you a lot longer to bring your mompreneur dream to life. Melissa Arnott, mother of six- and nine-year-old boys, is the owner of The BabyTime Shows, consumer shows geared towards new and expecting parents. She started her business while at work full-time. While she admits it took her longer to get it off the ground, she also had the luxury of really thinking about and honing her business model before she jumped in, all while bringing in a regular paycheque.

When your kids are very young

You've survived the sleepless nights (hopefully) and can now imagine juggling a business and your family. Or maybe you've had a couple of kids and returning to your old job no longer makes as much sense for your family. Whatever the reasons, lots of moms dip their toes into entrepreneurial waters when their kids are small. This is when Erica Ehm started the Yummy Mummy Club. Erica says, "I was despondent after my son was born. I don't like the feeling of my brain being turned off. I learned this from my first baby and did something about it after my second. I learned that the best thing for me to do is work."

The good news in this scenario is that you've got a bit of a handle on parenthood. You've gotten past "mommy brain." Your body has returned to something that at least resembles its original state. You probably also have some sort of childcare routine, whether the kids are home full-time or not. In short, you can focus on your business and you may even have a few hours to work on it.

We've heard it said many times that you can't start a business while your kids are sleeping. We say that you *can*, you just can't grow it quickly. If your kids are good sleepers, you just might have some good, dedicated work time every day. The bad news about starting a business with toddlers or preschoolers underfoot is that little kids can be unpredictable at best and downright unreasonable at worst.

Any mom can tell you that you're never more popular with your kids than when the phone rings, which is often when Junior decides to practise his best screaming. Small children also need a lot of attention, which can make it hard to really sink your teeth into whatever you're working on. If you're willing to put in a full day with your little kids and then get to work after they go to sleep, then starting a business when they're young might be the perfect timing for you. Just keep in mind that your work accomplishments between 9 a.m. and 5 p.m. may be sporadic.

When your kids are bigger

Your role as a parent is a moving target. We wouldn't say that parenting gets *easier* as your children grow, just different. The same holds true for your business—we'll come back to this later. We would say, though, that daily life is easier when everyone in the house wipes their own bums, drinks from a cup, and puts on their own shoes. So it makes a lot of sense that some great entrepreneurial ventures come to life when the kids are a bit bigger.

We love how Joni Lien, who launched SupperWorks, a meal preparation company, when her kids were bigger, describes being ready for a new phase: "It was time for me to not be at home, waiting for people to come home." Joni, and her business partner Chris, started SupperWorks when their kids (both are moms of two) were all in the double digits. Now they enjoy having their kids around the business, even employing them part-time.

While starting a business with older children affords you more time and concentration, it can also present challenges. Change doesn't always come easy to a household, and the sudden absence of mom is likely to be noticed. One mompreneur we spoke to told us that her teenage son had a really hard time with her starting to work. He felt her absence acutely. This mom recounts how difficult the stress on the relationship with her son was and tells us that she is still working to rebuild what they lost during that start-up time in her life.

This is but one story. Every family is going to react differently. The key is to find the time to start your business that works for you. It's never going to be the perfect time. Hopefully by now you're getting the idea that mompreneurship can be great, but you're never going to hear us use the word "perfect" when describing any aspect of it. It's like any other career move, with pluses and minuses for you to consider.

3

Things to look at before you leap

Is your life set up for self-employment?

Before you dive into your business venture, there are a few more things to think about. For starters, there are some practical considerations that may not have crossed your mind.

Is your nest full?

We'll talk more about the importance of thinking about a life plan, but before you even get to that point, ask yourself if you want more children. So many women we know have started their mom businesses while on the first maternity leave. Everything goes swimmingly until the second baby comes along. The second baby brings a whole load of change. We love those people who tell you that the second child is only twenty percent more work. Maybe in terms of food preparation and laundry . . . *maybe.* But as we've already mentioned, a second baby can be like a bomb dropped into your business, not to mention your household. We recommend spending some time thinking about how you will manage your business with more children. Will it still make sense from a financial point of view if you're paying for childcare for two, or three? Or can you work from home with several small children at your feet?

Who's counting on you?

As we wait longer to start our families, the phenomenon of the sandwich generation has come to the forefront. Women like us are caring for children and for aging parents simultaneously. (It seems that we're the jelly.) In the interest of your well-being, we want to remind you to think about all of the obligations in your life, not just your parenting obligations. If you have others who will depend on you in the years to come, you may want to think twice about starting your own business. This book should give you a sense of the enormous amount of work involved in getting a successful business off the ground. Even if all goes well you will be stunned at what is required. Your resolve will be tested time and again. You need to make sure you have the required reserves of energy and patience before you dive in.

How long can you go without a paycheque?

Common wisdom states that it takes at least a year or two for a new business to be profitable. Our rule of thumb is that for a mompreneur it can take even longer. Not to mention that being profitable and taking home a comfortable salary are only distantly related. (We'll get back to that later.) No matter how smart and energetic you are, and how brilliant your idea, you may be working part-time. Part-time hours mean part-time money. Period. We'll talk lots about making money in this book, but it's imperative that you have a sense of how long you can live without it. Nothing is going to be more frustrating than spending a year getting your incredible business off the ground only to have to return to work full-time at that point.

Some mompreneurs told us that the instability of earnings is one of the hardest things about the mompreneur experience. Gone are the days of receiving regular paycheques that came whether you actually earned them or not!

If your family is relying on you to bring in some serious cash within the first few years, you may want to start your business while still working at your day job. Or, you may want to save your pennies until you have a dedicated period of time to get things going.

Together with your spouse (if you have one), create a very thorough and realistic family budget. Not only will it help you get a sense of what you really spend, it'll be great practice for budgeting for your business. Decide together where you can skimp and for how long. What are you willing to go without? What is your spouse willing to give up to finance your dream? If you want our advice, prepare yourself for this conversation and maybe send the kids to Grandma's. Starting a business is a very important decision for the whole family and you'll want everyone to be able to focus on the matter at hand.

While you're thinking about your financial status, look beyond paying for groceries and electricity. Ask yourself how long you can go without a vacation or your own cash for small luxuries. While you're at it, check in with your spouse about his career ambitions. How secure is his job? We know of more than a few mompreneurs who have found themselves on the brink of financial ruin, and we wonder if some planning might have mitigated their situations. Clearly you can't anticipate everything that will happen or how you'll react to various hypothetical situations, but we strongly advise that you have a solid financial plan before even thinking about giving up access to a steady income.

What does your love life look like?

If you are a would-be mompreneur who has a life partner or spouse, ask yourself how stable your romantic situation is. We're certain that behind every successful mompreneur is a great husband. (We've used the words *spouse* and *husband* throughout this book mainly for ease of clarity and distinction between a business partner and a life partner. If wife, girlfriend, boyfriend, plaything, etc., are more meaningful to you, then please insert the relevant term.) You will need your spouse more than you can imagine. He will be there to listen to your stresses and successes. He will support you emotionally and financially. If he's like our husbands, he'll build things, drag things, analyze things, and generally give a damn. We promise you, whether you have business partners or go it alone, your spouse is getting into this business with you.

Even if you're in a stable and healthy relationship, a new business can bring new stresses to the homestead. Several of the mompreneurs we talked to spoke of the tension it brought to their marriages. One mompreneur told us, "The business has definitely put a strain on our marriage. I was working a lot, and we were strapped financially. Since he was the only one earning an income the burden fell to him. I think it was natural he'd get a bit bitter about it. He was more impatient about the money than me—he'd say, 'When are you going to start making money?'"

But we don't want to give the impression that it's all negative—it absolutely isn't. Take a look at what Paula Jubinville, the business coach behind Aqueous, says: "My husband is delighted—he sees four hundred percent more of me now than he did in the first five years of my business. I'm not as stressed out—I'm doing what I like. He's proud—he shares in my accomplishments."

Before jumping into entrepreneurial waters you need to have a real, honest, and possibly tough conversation with your spouse. If you want him on board (and you do, trust us) he'll need to understand why you want to become a mompreneur, what you hope to achieve, and what you think are reasonable goals for your family and the business. Such a conversation took place in each of our households in early 2002. Our husbands were able to express their concerns and had the opportunity to weigh in and ultimately get behind our plan.

In truth, most spouses are incredibly supportive and proud. Countless mompreneurs we spoke to told us that their husbands believe in them even more than they believe in themselves. The point is that if your relationship is on the wobbly side, we might suggest waiting until you're in a more certain position. The last thing you want is to be waist-deep in a new business while going through a divorce.

Is help at hand?

One thing every mompreneur needs is a solid circle of family and friends who will help with everything from pep talks to childcare to schlepping. When we asked mompreneurs what they couldn't run their businesses without, they overwhelmingly they said their husbands, mothers, and friends.

Melissa Arnott, the force behind The BabyTime Shows, couldn't imagine running her business without her mom. Melissa's mom answers the phone, does the books, and generally makes Melissa's life possible. Even if you can't imagine working that closely with a relative, we can pretty much guarantee you're going to need help on some front, and a strong network of support will make all the difference.

Admiral Road, too, has been made possible by the generous support of loving family and friends who have collected and cared for our children in a pinch. While we've always planned to be with our kids part-time, business can be unpredictable and sometimes we need to call in reinforcements. We've also depended on the help of friends and family who have spread the word, come up with brilliant ideas, brought healthy snacks to trade shows, and so much more. Businesses have a way of taking on a life of their own—so a good support system is indispensable. We know we couldn't keep all of the balls in the air without our "team" and, of course, our husbands.

Beyond these practical considerations are some things that fall into the emotional or "knowing yourself" category.

What do you want your life to look like?

For many of us, the whole point of being a mompreneur is to have some control over our lives. So take the time up front to figure out what it is you want out of your life. This is true for everyone, but perhaps most for mompreneurs.

You can't be happy unless you take all aspects of your life into consideration. Spend the time figuring out what you really want your life to be like—that will ground you in all your decisions. Visualize what you want your family and work to be like.

—Paula Jubinville, Aqueous

Maybe you want to work two days a week, or maybe you want to work full-time. Maybe you want to be very focused on your business, or maybe you just want to dabble. In our books it doesn't much matter what your vision is, just so long as you have one.

In our case, we knew that we didn't want to work a hundred hours a week. We wanted the opportunity to be there not just for our kids, but for the other parts of our lives as well. Now there are months in the year when we worry our kids might forget what we look like and when the idea of getting to the gym is laughable, but having a clear idea of what our ideal life-business balance is helps immeasurably. We wanted to be home with our kids when they were very small and available to them at all times if they needed us. But we didn't want to be full-time moms. We were looking for something in the middle from our lives. We've planned and run our business accordingly. It hasn't been a get-rich quick plan. (Remember what we said you earn when you just work part-time?) But it's been exactly what we envisioned for our lives. And it has allowed us to stay with our business long enough to grow it.

Victoria Turner is a mom of three kids under five and owner of Pippalily and Simply on Board, companies that make baby slings and accessories. Victoria explains her choice this way: "I wanted to run my business, not have my business run me. I'm not a Type A personality and I didn't want to have a crazy business life."

Other mompreneurs have a different perspective. Sarah Morgenstern, one of the two women behind SavvyMom.ca, an online resource for moms, tells us, "My objectives were not about work-life balance. I don't work fewer hours now." Like we said, it's all in the motivation.

Are you okay with what you'll be missing?

Getting off the corporate career track can be very exciting and empowering. It can also be fraught with anxiety. Not only does a mompreneur leave behind the security of a paycheque and the camaraderie of co-workers, she also leaves behind an easy-to-follow career path. Now, it'll be up to you to track your own progress. No career reviews and promotions for you. You'll also watch as your former colleagues, as well as friends, family, and spouse, climb their career ladders.

What will it be like for you to watch your peers and partner advance in their careers while you have stepped out of the corporate world? We've honestly never missed our downtown jobs—in fact our chests tighten if we get within a half-mile of the downtown corporate corridor. But there have been twinges of something related to envy when our former colleagues and classmates have received promotions and opportunities. Ultimately it all comes back to your life vision. We know that the price of a high-powered corporate career and all the trimmings was too high for us and our families—but that doesn't mean the grass doesn't look green over there from time to time.

Can you stomach risk?

With any business comes a degree of risk. What if it doesn't work out? There's the possibility of losing your monetary investment, but there's also a possibility of damage to your self-confidence and even your relationships.

If you're starting any business, you're going to have to assume at least a little financial risk. We know mompreneurs who started their businesses for a few hundred dollars, and others for half a million dollars.

Historically, women entrepreneurs have gotten a bad rap for being risk-averse. And we'll admit it—we are guilty as charged. We invested a relatively small amount of money up front—basically an amount that we felt comfortable losing. We had walked away from big salaries and knew from the get-go that we would likely never replace the income we could have made had we stayed on the corporate track. In short, we weren't primarily motivated by money.

Many of our mompreneur colleagues share a similar perspective where risk is concerned. Alison Kramer of Nummies says, "I think you have to be a little risk-averse. I never wanted to take on a lot of debt. I wanted to be able to walk away from my business if I had to."

HOW MARS AND VENUS VIEW GROWTH

Dr. Barbara Orser has spent a lot of time thinking about and researching the differences between men and women entrepreneurs. Her research indicates that women approach entrepreneurship for lots of reasons besides financial motivation. Women are less likely to take on debt in their business. Here's what she has to say about the difference in desire for growth: "Where women differ from their male counterparts is how they view growth. Women business owners view growth to be less important, less likely, and of lower value than men. They view the personal demands related to growth as negative and adding stress to their lives. An overwhelming eighty-four percent of women feel their business has reached a size they are comfortable with and don't want to grow. This compared to thirty-seven percent for men."

So how much should you invest? Here's the thing—if you only invest a little money, then chances are you'll only make a little money. You've heard the old adage—you've got to spend money to make money. So if you're setting out to make your millions, then you'll likely need to invest a significant amount. There are entrepreneurial groups for women who work hard to promote "thinking big" among female entrepreneurs. The wisdom is that it takes just as much effort to start a big business as it does a small one.

Victoria Sopik of Kids & Company has this to say about her tolerance for risk: "I didn't worry about the risk. It's only money. It's idiotic to put yourself in business and then go crazy worrying about money. You have to decide what you want to invest and what you're willing to lose and why. Then you have to pull the plug if you have to if it's not working."

The advantage of starting out big is the enormous potential you have to make money. Any business person will tell you that the only way you can accrue serious wealth is to own the company. And while the downside may be significant, there's usually something to be learned from a failed business.

So should you go big or go home? It's up to you, of course, to decide if you have the stomach for taking a big leap. If you're scared to go for it, know that even a small cottage industry has complexities you can't yet imagine. No matter how much you invest or how big you want to grow, you will have trials, tribulations, achievements, and aggravations. There is definitely a good case for risking bigger for bigger payoffs.

On the other hand, even if you have a big company, it doesn't necessarily mean you're making money. As Danielle's husband likes to remind us, for many of the years we've been in business, we've made more money than Ford Motor Company! At the end of the day you need to be mindful of the fact that a large proportion of new businesses fail. So whether you think big and bet it all or decide to keep your risk and your potential smaller, be prepared to lose what you're investing.

Do you have the right stuff?

A lot has been written about what it takes to be a successful entrepreneur. Many people suggest that you're either a born entrepreneur or you're not. The search for entrepreneurial personality traits has gone on for ages, with no concrete findings. The issue is that many of the characteristics of successful entrepreneurs are also those of successful people in most fields, and are not particular to people who start a commercial enterprise.

Over time, many people have compiled lists of entrepreneurial traits. We took a crack at it too, and here's the checklist we came up with:

- ❏ Hard work
- ❏ Risk taking
- ❏ Creativity
- ❏ Flexibility
- ❏ Multi-tasking
- ❏ Self-confidence
- ❏ Self-motivation
- ❏ Willingness to learn
- ❏ Patience
- ❏ Ability to handle and learn from criticism
- ❏ Ability to learn from mistakes

We know that you're checking off the personality traits at this very moment. Here's a suggestion: ask a number of people you know to answer honestly whether or not you have these traits. We are all wonderfully responsible, hard-working, able to handle criticism, etc., right? The truth is that you probably have lots of these characteristics, but not all of them. So do you need all or any of these traits? The answer, we think, is qualified. Yes, you will benefit immensely from starting out with many of these traits. Of course you need to be a hard worker—there will be no shortage of work. And yes, you will need to be self-directed and independent—if not you, then who else will get this business off the ground?

Of the women we surveyed, almost all (over eighty percent) described themselves as self-motivated and willing to learn. Being creative, as well as able to get things done in a chaotic environment, also ranked high. However, fewer than half described themselves as patient and just fifty percent said they were able to handle rejection.

So what happens if you don't have all of these traits? Well, for one thing, we think you'll learn some of these skills on the job. For example, maybe you're not great with criticism now, but if you or any of your customers happen to be human, we can pretty much guarantee someone, sometime will have something not so nice to say. You will learn from this. We have received a surprisingly small number of complaints over the years—but we have received a few. We used to go nutty over them. Over time we've learned to hear the criticism and either act on it or dismiss it without getting too wound up. We now try to treat all feedback, good or bad, as information. In other words, this is a trait we've acquired.

Another way around not being pure entrepreneurial material is to have a partner. If you're missing some key entrepreneurial characteristics, it just may be that your partner has it covered. In fact, in most cases where businesses are jointly started by more than one person, it's for this very reason. And, if you don't have a partner, you can always hire smartly and outsource your real weaknesses.

Many of the mompreneurs we spoke to told us that they relied heavily on employees and subcontractors to do the things they aren't naturally suited to. Things like bookkeeping and web services are natural tasks for outsourcing, but sales, marketing, and more can also be outsourced if it makes sense for your business. The trick is to make sure that you are spending your time to the greatest advantage of the business.

Ultimately, it is worth thinking about whether you have what it takes to run your own business. It could save you some pain down the road. But determining whether you've got what it takes by ticking off boxes on a checklist alone makes about as much sense as determining the future of your relationship by taking a Cosmo quiz. Be honest with yourself. If you want to go for it, then by all means, we want you to jump in. We just want you to do it with your eyes open. And remember, if the timing isn't right just now, your entrepreneurial spirit doesn't have an expiration date. Where there's a will, there's a way.

PART 2

CONCEPTION:
COMING UP WITH YOUR IDEA

There are many similarities between conceiving your business and conceiving a real, live baby: you can approach either act in many different ways, but ultimately, a number of things need to be in place to make sure that your dream becomes a reality. Now that you're considering mompreneurship, the next question you'll want to ask yourself is, "What kind of business is for me?" Here we'll help you tackle how to come up with an idea that suits you. (And unlike making a baby, you get to choose exactly how you want your business to look!)

4

The world is your oyster

What business is for you?

There are various ways you can get to working for yourself—from direct sales to.buying a business to starting from scratch. And even if you don't have a clue what it is you want to do, you can still get to your Big Idea, we promise.

When we asked the mompreneurs for their best advice about starting a business, many of them answered, "Be passionate!" and "Love what you do!" We can honestly tell you, this just wasn't the case for us. We were motivated not by the idea of making baby blankets but by the idea of striking out on our own and charting a new path for ourselves. We were passionate about finding a business that suited us—not necessarily that we were passionate about. That being said, if you have a fabulous idea that you've always wanted to pursue, then we hope we can help you out in another way: just pass "Go," collect your $200, and proceed to "Assessing the viability of a business" on page 73.

Or, maybe you are converting an existing career into an entrepreneurial venture. Maybe you're a marketing whiz or a public relations pro or a graphic designer and you're looking for a way to take control of your career and launch yourself into self-employment. If this is the case, congratulations! You've conceived, and you can go directly to the business planning stage. (We'd like to think that you might find something interesting along the way, but if you're impatient to get started, go ahead and skip this section— we forgive you!)

But for the legions of you who are out there, yearning to start your own businesses but lacking the Big Idea, this section is for you.

In the next chapter we'll discuss techniques for developing your business idea, including brainstorming, developing a personal list of criteria, evaluating your idea, and knowing how to ask yourself the right questions. But before we get there, let's touch on a few other ways you can become a self-employed mom. With these options, you'll still have to determine whether one of them will work for you, but you won't have to do all the legwork of starting something from scratch.

Reinvent an old career

No doubt, when you choose to become self-employed there is a huge learning curve. That being said, we spoke to many mompreneurs who drew on their past professional experience to launch themselves into entrepreneurship.

WeeHands is an international company offering sign language classes to young children. But it didn't start out that way. It actually began in Sara Bingham's dining room. When Sara worked in the field of language development, she signed with preschoolers. When she became a mom, she began signing with her own kids. Once she started, she realized, "This is what I'm supposed to be doing." Today WeeHands is the world's leading children's sign language and language development program for babies and preschoolers. The company boasts over fifty instructors teaching classes across North America.

Samantha Linton, who creates and markets erotica for women,

used her skills and contacts from her television producing career to write, produce, cast, and direct her video. Of her experience she says, "Each step in my career has groomed me for this business. There was no aspect of self-employment that daunted me because I had touched on everything in my professional career."

Many women told us similar stories—that they took the skills they acquired in the corporate world and applied them to their entrepreneurial venture.

Even if you can't reinvent or recycle your professional career in your new venture, you sure can take your experience and reuse it. Think about the myriad skills you possess and how you can apply them in your new dream gig. You might just have an asset you can trade upon.

Join an existing company

There are several ways that you can have your own "business within a business," and many of these are great options for moms. In some instances, like direct sales, you can test the waters of entrepreneurship without assuming a huge financial risk. In other options, like franchising, the financial commitment can be significant. But there's an upside. You don't need to come up with the great business idea or brand. Someone's already done that for you. Each of these options requires a varying commitment of time and money, so let's look at each a little more closely and see what mompreneurs have to say about them.

Direct sales

When you work for a direct sales company, you market and sell products directly to your customers—often through home parties.

There are no brick-and-mortar stores. There are two ways to make money: commissions from how much product you sell and incentives based on how many new salespeople you recruit to the company. Some direct sales companies you may be familiar with include Discovery Toys, Mary Kay Cosmetics, and the Pampered Chef.

In a nutshell, the pros for starting your own direct sales business include low start-up costs (typically a couple hundred dollars), complete flexibility about how, when, and where you work, and often a quality product to sell. You don't need to source products or conduct market research because the company has done that for you. You'll also enjoy the support of a large company's marketing and branding efforts. Most direct sales companies also offer sales incentives such as jewellery and vacations.

The downside to direct sales that we have heard most frequently is that it is actually hard to make money. And it's REALLY hard to make a lot of money. This is not for the shy girl! Your sales skills should be strong—or at the very least, you should be enthusiastic. And you have to be willing to solicit business from your friends, family, colleagues—and from one mompreneur we know—strangers in the supermarket. You also may be required to recruit other salespeople to the company. We've seen many women join direct sales companies when their children are very young. Let's face it— it's a relatively low-risk way to be engaged in a constructive project before your mind goes numb from watching one too many *Blue's Clues* episodes. But having young kids is a pretty big distraction to your business, and if you've only invested a few hundred dollars, your commitment to getting it off the ground might be low. At the outset, these mompreneurs enjoy and benefit from the product they're selling. Often, however, we've seen their businesses peter out after they've exhausted sales with their immediate social circles.

Direct sales is a great option if you're looking for a small, part-time business with no risk. Or if you have great sales skills and a lot of discipline, but don't want to reinvent the wheel.

For $140, you can become an educational consultant for Discovery Toys. Your start-up kit includes sample educational toys for home parties, business tools, and supplies to start your business, and a free personal website. Educational consultants enjoy a minimum twenty percent commission on their sales, as well as bonuses for signing up new team members and opportunities to earn family vacations.

You can join cosmetics giant Mary Kay for about $130. A starter kit includes lots of cosmetic samples and a "how-to business guide." You'll earn fifty percent of everything you sell, but you'll have to pay for your own website and purchase at least $800 in inventory a year.

For as little as $80, you can become a consultant for the Pampered Chef. Your new consultant kit will include products, catalogues, training materials, business management software, and business supplies. You'll earn at least twenty percent of your sales through "cooking shows"—home parties where you share recipes and cooking techniques.

Hyla Pollak is a mother of four teenagers who owns Gemini Consulting, which helps companies sell and market their products through network marketing. Before starting Gemini, she spent many years with Discovery Toys and became very senior in the company. To be successful at direct sales, Hyla believes you really have to love your product, and she LOVED Discovery Toys. "I couldn't have done it otherwise," she says. As a result of her sales and recruitment efforts, she won many trips and items that she and her family enjoyed.

You can check out the Direct Sellers Association where you live if you want to learn more about these kinds of business opportunities.

FIVE DOs AND DON'Ts FROM A DIRECT SALES EXPERT

1. DO love the product you want to sell. If you're using it and loving it, your enthusiasm will show.
2. DO plan "office hours" where you can be focused on work and not have to worry about other "stuff" in your life.
3. DO find a buddy in the business. This is someone you can share your goals with and challenge each other to reach each goal you set.
4. DO touch your business each and every day, whether it's making phone calls or sharing what you love with people you meet throughout your busy day.
5. DO attend meetings, listen to training calls, and stay in contact with all of your teammates. There is a great saying in direct sales—if your business is slow, you need the meeting. If your business is booming, the meeting needs you!

1. DON'T spend money and time "playing office." Only spend money on things that will *earn* you money!
2. DON'T think that business will just fall into your lap. Go after it! Network!
4. DON'T stay in your comfort zone and expect growth. Growth happens only when you can step outside the box. Not asking is a guaranteed No.
4. DON'T buy a lot of inventory. No one will be happy with a home full of unused products.
5. DON'T give up. Remember that there's only one degree difference between hot water and boiling water. If you turn the heat off at ninety-nine degrees, you'll never reach boiling point.

—Hyla Pollak, Gemini Consulting

Licensing

Many successful mompreneur businesses offer opportunities to join their teams without having to assume all the risk of starting a company from scratch. Mom-oriented fitness programs, baby-friendly movie-going, and sign language classes are some of the businesses we've seen crop up with licensee programs. For a nominal cost, you can purchase the right to use an established company's brand and product while running your own show. You can set your own schedule and manage your own business while enjoying the support of the parent company. Licensing is an "eat what you kill" model: You pay a small amount to use the company's product. After you've earned back your initial investment, the subsequent cash earned is yours to keep. A license has to be renewed annually if the licensee wants to continue to promote her business and use the parent company's material and brand.

Robyn Green-Ruskin, mother of two small boys and founder of Movies for Mommies, never anticipated that people would want to license her business. Robyn offers baby-friendly movie screenings: the volume is turned down for sensitive baby ears, change tables and bottle warming are available, and no one will give you a nasty look when your baby cries. After she received national media exposure, people caught on. So when Robyn was approached by women interested in licensing her business, she drew on her past professional experience to launch a licensing program. Robyn cautions that licensing is not necessarily a sure thing.

Robyn says, "I now know how to recognize who is going to be a successful licensee. In entrepreneurship, there are no guarantees. You have to take a leap of faith—otherwise you should get a nine-to-five job. I give my licensees the recipe for the cake, but I don't tell them how to make it."

Licensing offers you a degree of support while letting you run with your own ideas about how to succeed.

WHAT YOU GET WHEN YOU BECOME A LICENSEE

On average, initial licensing fees run between $500 and a few thousand dollars. At WeeHands, for example, once you are accepted as a qualified instructor, your annual license enables you to market and teach your own WeeHands-branded baby sign language classes. Licensees pay an annual licensing fee of $150. This allows the use of WeeHands copyrighted and trademarked materials, as well as support and professional development from the company. WeeHands instructors also have to purchase the curricula they want to teach. Each curriculum has a fee of about $150.

Franchise

Purchasing a franchise is a unique opportunity to be in business for yourself but not by yourself. This is considered to be one of the biggest advantages over slogging it out on your own. What does it mean to own a franchise? You (the franchisee) have bought—often for several hundred thousand dollars—the right to sell a company's product or service in a certain location from the franchisor. And, in most cases, the franchisee pays an ongoing royalty fee to the franchisor. The franchisee has to follow certain rules established by the franchisor. Unlike a license, a franchise is typically a more rigid scenario with little opportunity to personalize the business. Familiar franchises include McDonald's, Pizza Hut, and Tim Hortons.

Here's the skinny on franchises: There are three advantages of buying a franchise over starting from scratch. First, you are buying an established corporate image. Your customers will already be familiar with and have trust in your brand. Second, the franchisor trains and supports the franchisee. You won't necessarily find these kinds of resources if you're striking out on your own. Finally, you'll be able to get the ball rolling quickly. Since the franchise company already has a business model firmly in place, you'll save time in the start-up phase, allowing you to focus on running your business.

Common wisdom also says there are three strikes against buying a franchise: First, there are no guarantees. You can invest a ton of money, but the franchisor cannot promise you success. Second is a loss of control. We've come across plenty of Type A entrepreneurs who want to do it all, but as a franchisee, you are bound to follow the systems that have been put in place by the franchisor and need permission to make changes. Finally, if there is conflict between the franchisee and franchisor, things can go south pretty quickly.

The mompreneurs we talked to who had first-hand experience with franchises told us this: Do your homework and have a good rapport with the franchisor—this needs to be someone you can have a relationship with. Ask yourself if you can work with this person in the long-term. Also, know that buying a franchise is not a slam dunk. There is risk involved and you will have to build your business. You need to evaluate your own skill set and ask yourself the right questions.

Like everything else we're suggesting here, know what you want to get out of your business. For example, if you have excellent management skills but aren't an "ideas" person, a franchise might be an excellent option. Managing people, money, processes, and systems are prerequisites for successful franchisees. (Whereas the thrill of creating something new might turn the crank of someone else.)

There's a reason franchising has been around for a long time. It's a great way to own and operate your own business. If you're thinking about buying a franchise, do your research—on the company and yourself—get some legal advice, and make sure you read the fine print.

The average franchise fee runs from $20,000 to $30,000. You will also pay ongoing royalty fees, which are generally a percentage of your sales. Your initial investment will vary greatly depending on the industry and type of business you're interested in. These start-up costs can be relatively low (less than $20,000) or very pricey (over $1 million). According to the International Franchise Association, the average investment is between $350,000 and $400,000. A Tim Hortons franchise costs approximately $450,000.

If you're interested in more information about buying a franchise, you can contact the Canadian Franchise Association or the franchise association where you live.

Buy an existing business

A strong argument for buying a business instead of starting one is the existence of a track record. When you buy a business, you have a sense of what it has done in the past and therefore what it's likely to do in the future. You also get to skip all the hiccups associated with a start-up and benefit from what has already been learned. Think of it as being handed a child without the fun of conception or the chaos of living with a newborn.

Buying a business can be a great way to leapfrog into entrepreneurship. Although some of the mompreneurs we know bought their businesses, we wouldn't say that this is a typical path. Jumping into an existing business could place more demands on your time than slowly building one from scratch. On the other hand, there's nothing wrong with existing cash flow!

With the aging of baby boomers, there is expected to be a big increase in the number of entrepreneurs wanting to sell their businesses in the next decade. There may be some great opportunities to buy a ready-made business.

—Prof. Reuber

We told you earlier about Jan Frolic, the dynamo behind Magazine Network, a media sales company. Buying a business was Jan's way into entrepreneurship. She began working for the company in her twenties because she needed a job. At the time, she was married but didn't have children or own a home. As it turned out, Jan was a rock star in sales. After a few years, another company tried to headhunt her away. Jan took a chance and offered to buy the company instead of leaving. The owner was ready to move on with his career and accepted Jan's offer. She bought him out and within two years the company was hers. Jan was successful because she knew the job, knew the company, and had no other demands on her time.

Buy an existing business: Our story

Not many people know it, but this is also the path we chose. Not that it's a secret—it's just that our business today looks very different from the one we purchased eight years ago. But this is in fact how we chose to start.

When we were first thinking about starting a business, it seemed like everyone we knew was having a baby, and we were in the market for a lot of baby gifts. A friend told us about a company in a small town that made personalized baby blankets. They were the ideal baby gift: reasonably priced, beautifully handmade to spec, and delivered to the new mom's front door. Naturally, we began to buy them for our child-bearing friends. But then one day Amy heard that the company wasn't making blankets anymore. After laying out and evaluating all of our criteria for entrepreneurship (more on that in a moment), we realized that this business was a perfect fit. So, we took a deep breath and called the business owner directly to see if she'd be interested in selling her company.

The owner, Betty, had a brick-and-mortar gift store in cottage country. She fell into making baby blankets quite accidentally. She made one for a friend, and it was so well received that her husband suggested she sell them. When she marketed the blankets, they unexpectedly took off. By the time we called her, however, she had discontinued production. She simply couldn't find anyone who could sew for her.

When we spoke to Betty, we asked if she would be interested in selling the assets of her company. She had a sewing machine, a cutting table, and finished blankets just taking up space. She had paid for those assets but now had no outlet for them. (Can you imagine getting a call out of the blue from someone offering you money to take away your old junk? It would be like winning the lottery.)

That being said, the assets weren't worth much. The price was right—and for a few thousand dollars plus legal fees, a blanket business was ours. We rented a van to drive up to cottage country, hauled away a bunch of stuff, and turned our thoughts to our new venture.

(By the way, we experienced a small blip before the deal was sealed. After we arrived in town, Betty sprung some news on us. In her storage room were several rolls of fabric that she never used up and no longer had any use for. Betty insisted that we pay for and take the fabric with us—fabric we had no intention of using. She announced that we couldn't run a blanket business without fleece. We were furious. We felt like Betty was pulling a fast one on us and we actually walked away from the bargaining table! We headed to the only local greasy spoon around to discuss our options. Although we weren't thrilled with the new assets we were about to acquire, we decided to bite the bullet and buy the fabric. It seems silly now, but spending that extra $500 didn't seem so funny at the time.)

Although the Admiral Road of today bears little resemblance to the company we bought, there *were* some great advantages to buying the business. We didn't need to reinvent the wheel. For starters, we knew there was a market for this product because we had been customers ourselves. We also knew that these personalized blankets were terrific—they washed well, held up to the abuses only a baby can dish out, and were loved by kids and parents alike.

Of course it occurred to us that we could have started our own personalized blanket company without buying Betty's business. Heck, given that she was no longer making the blankets, we could have ripped off the designs ourselves. But from Day One, this is not how we wanted to do business. The fact is that we did not own those designs and they did not belong to us until we bought them. We didn't want to start out borrowing from someone else any more than we want to imitate another company today. As you'll read later in the book, we don't think a mompreneur should ever rip off another mom.

We also sent out a mailing to her customer list. We used all of her suppliers (wholesale fabric distributors, packing boxes, bags, thread). It would have taken us months to source everything on our own. Betty helped us work out our cost structure. Despite being newly minted MBAs, we didn't have a clue about how to price our product. But Betty was a retail expert and she willingly shared her knowledge with us. We applied to the same craft show she participated in and had a benchmark of what kind of sales to expect. We learned from Betty that craft shows would be an effective way to market our product, and they always have been.

Ultimately, buying a business requires many factors to come together, and in our observation it's fairly uncommon in the world of mompreneurs. But if you are interested in this route, try speaking to a business broker. This is someone who can help you conduct a search for a business, evaluate opportunities, and negotiate a purchase. You can search for brokers online. If you do have an opportunity to buy a business that meets your personal and financial criteria, it can be a great way to start. It worked for us!

5

The Big Idea

Starting your business from scratch

In our travels, we've talked to women who built maternity shops, baby boutiques, and book stores. We've met women who invented products such as bibs, barrettes, and baby food. How about nursing bras or crawling pants or a magazine? Or online stores, online newsletters, and online communities? The list goes on and on. Actually, most of the mompreneurs we know of started their businesses from scratch. Some of these mompreneurs had prior business experience, and some had none at all. What binds this diverse group is that they all had an "aha" moment, when they realized exactly what it was they should be doing. These next chapters will take you through the process of how you too can get to your Big Idea. We applied the methods taught to us by Professor Rebecca Reuber during our MBA years that helped us come up with the right business for us. It worked for us, so we're sharing it with you.

Brainstorming

Sometimes the very idea of brainstorming makes us shudder. Flash-backs to cheesy group facilitators with flip charts in our corporate pasts spring to mind. But guess what? Brainstorming really works. And now that the goal is about finding yourself a business idea instead of solving someone else's corporate woes, you just might be more motivated than when you were in the meeting room. We've all heard the expression "no idea is a bad one" in brainstorming, and it's true. But now, instead of sitting around a meeting room table, you're probably on your own. That's okay. Just start by writing down every idea you can think of. Ask your friends and relatives for their ideas—use your imagination! The goal here is to generate as many possible ideas as you can.

When it came time to conceive our business idea, we followed this exercise. The process of figuring out the best option for us took some time. This is not an exercise that needs to be completed during your baby's afternoon nap. We were completely methodical. We literally sat around for weeks tossing out different ideas. We hashed them out with our friends, our family, even our hairdressers.

Think about everything you've ever thought was wrong with the world, every product you wish you had, every product you have but wish was better, every service your neighbourhood is missing, etc. Here are some broad categories to think about.

There's a hole in the market, dear Liza, dear Liza . . .

Some women we know started thinking about their businesses by noticing what was missing from their lives. These realizations often evolved over a long (or long-ish) period of time.

Victoria Turner, the creator of Pippalily, a company that makes baby slings and accessories, had a light bulb moment with her business idea. According to Victoria, "I had fully intended to be a stay-at-home mom. My baby wanted to be held all the time and I was using a very generic baby sling that someone had given me. People asked me about it all the time. I was on a flight to Halifax and three different people asked me about the sling, and I said to my husband, 'I have to do something about this.' We started making notes on that flight." Today, Pippalily products, as well as products from Victoria's second brand, are found in stores around the world.

And there is Lisa Will, founder of Stonz, which makes outdoor gear for kids. Lisa had been actively looking for a business idea when opportunity knocked. She says, "I have a love of the outdoors and continued that love affair with my newborn son. We were spending time outside and his feet were freezing! I looked everywhere but couldn't find any warm footwear for babies. Then I bumped into an old friend and his family. His wife had made her own warm booties for her kids. I recognized a gaping hole in the market. I approached her about building a business together."

Have a look around—maybe you can identify a hole in a market.

Just do it . . . better

Some women learned about an existing business idea but thought that they could improve upon it.

Despite the fact that she's a mom to two boys, Sundi Hoffman is the founder of a very girly business. She began designing barrettes with a girlfriend for her daughter. The two women took the barrettes to a few small shows and they sold well. With a background in sales, Sundi convinced a sales rep to take on the barrettes on a trial basis. In four months, her company, Bugalug, had products in nearly one hundred stores. Granted, Sundi didn't invent the hair barrette. But here's her take on how she brainstormed her way to a better barrette: "I decided I wanted to be the best no-slip clip on the market. One night my husband and I stayed up to brainstorm the best way to get the clip to not slip. We had a few drinks and then we went into the garage and tried everything we could think of to get the barrettes to stay in place. It was five in the morning and we were finally getting ready for bed when I had my 'aha' moment: the silicone on my pull-up stockings! I quickly cut up the stockings and made a pair of barrettes and we each put one in our hair. When the barrettes were still in our hair when we woke up in the morning, I knew that I had found a winner."

So when you're trying to come up with your business idea, you may not have to *reinvent* the wheel. Just find a way to make it work better.

Just do it . . . elsewhere

Other women recognize a great business opportunity by seeing it work successfully elsewhere. This was the case for Chris Wood and Joni Lien who started SupperWorks—a brick-and-mortar meal-prep store that provides the materials to make assembling dinners quick and easy. The customer chooses the dishes she wants to make and the store does the chopping, dicing, grating, and washing of the necessary ingredients. You follow the instructions, freeze the dinners at home, and defrost and cook them as needed. Sound good? It gets even better: Chris and Joni say that this is even more fun when done with a girlfriend or two and a glass of wine in hand.

According to Chris, "Being laid off from my job at the bank was the biggest gift of my life. I wanted to do something that really spoke to me—and that wasn't the case at my bank job. When I first read about meal preparation as a business in a U.S. magazine, my jaw dropped. I couldn't stop thinking about it. When I told my friend Joni about it, she couldn't stop thinking about it either. We said, 'Let's do this.'" SupperWorks burst onto the scene as Canada's first meal-prep company. Today it's in fifteen locations and growing fast.

Turn your passion into a business

Some women we know have been lucky enough to marry a passion or long-time hobby with a business idea.

Jennifer Torres, founder of Salsa Babies, found her Big Idea in her favourite hobby. She says, "One of my friends suggested that I marry my love of salsa with motherhood and create a baby salsa class. I was negative on the idea at first. The idea sat with me a while and I came around on it."

Jennifer Salter of Lifeline Personal Training found a way to marry her passions of psychotherapy and counselling, fitness, and the outdoors. "After I broke my neck in a biking accident, I felt that I could relate to people with special medical needs. I was really interested in that area. Now many of my fitness clients are people with special medical needs."

Ideas, ideas, ideas. That's the goal of brainstorming. And hey, at the end of the day you only need one great idea. Keep going—if you will it, it will come.

Develop a list of criteria

Now that you've got a pile of different business ideas, it's time to make a different kind of list: your criteria. This has nothing to do with what *type* of business you will have, but rather what *kind* of business it will be. Your criteria will dictate your decisions down the road. Criteria will include how much money is available to start up, how much time you have available given your family obligations, and what expertise you hold. Other important considerations are your tolerance for risk and whether you want to work alone or with a partner.

Since a rule of thumb is that it often takes entrepreneurs several years before they draw a salary from their business, you'll want to ask yourself things like, "Will I be happy working in this business in three years' time? In five? For free?" And we've talked about the fact that when you're working on your business part-time, it might take even longer until you're able to draw a salary. Other considerations include: What will your family look like down the road? At what stage will your kids be?

Mompreneur Paula Jubinville and her business partner took the time to develop their criteria from the start. Paula says, "My business partner was adamant up front about what she wanted—the number of hours, the timing. It was great. It gave us a blueprint for going forward. We were clear about who we were as an employer. We were picky about our clients."

This is also a time to imagine how big you want to grow your business. Eryn Green, a former management consultant, and Tamar Wagman, a former event planner, went big from the get-go by founding baby food company Sweetpea Baby Food and Organic Snacks. These mompreneurs say, "We wanted to build an empire and we still do. We never wanted to be small—we knew we couldn't ever make money unless we went big."

What we're getting at is that there is a wide range of criteria when starting a business, and they are as varied as the women behind the projects. Whatever your particular motivations and limitations, it certainly isn't going to hurt to think hard about them at the outset.

Now, evaluate your ideas against your criteria

Don't be alarmed, but when you begin to match your business ideas against your criteria, you will eliminate most of your ideas. If you have to, go back to the drawing board. Keep going until you've got a couple of ideas that fit your criteria.

When we were brainstorming, one idea that stuck around for a little while was a downtown spa. We had both worked in office towers and, at the time, there was nowhere to pop in for a lunchtime mani-pedi. We had identified the need for this business, but when we matched it against our criteria—low cost being at the top of the list—we had to nix it. We just weren't prepared to borrow the hundreds of thousands of dollars to bring that vision to reality. Plus we had the realization that it would behoove us to go to aesthetician school—something that just wasn't going to happen at that point.

Your criteria don't have to be extensive. For Nicole Garza it turned out to be one pretty simple idea. Although Nicole had no prior business experience, she now owns Mally Designs, the original leather bib company that sells its product in hundreds of retail stores. One day when feeding her baby, some food spilled onto the leather shoe her child was wearing. A simple wipe with a cloth was all it took—the spill easily wiped away like magic. It was at that moment that the idea of leather bibs was born. Nicole says, "Someone once told me that in order for your business to be successful, your product needs to be different. It needs to be worth talking about. Even before I had my 'lucky spill,' I carried that thought around with me in the back of my mind."

We have worked with our graphic designer, Mandy Webster, for years. One of the reasons we were drawn to work with Mandy is that she too is a mompreneur. Even though Mandy didn't intend to start out in graphic design, when she eventually matched her idea with her criteria, she was in business. Mandy explains: "My professional background is in both design and copywriting, but I planned to be a stay-at-home mom. I had been accepted into a government course that taught entrepreneurship. In order to qualify for the course you needed to do a serious business proposal. My idea for the course was to open a coffee shop that was friendly to mothers, but in creating the proposal I saw that this was impractical—and I needed an idea, so I came up with this graphic design business. I had designed a logo as a favour for a friend, and then for a few more friends, so I could see making a living at it. Doing the proposal got my creative juices flowing and I began to see the possibilities. At the time I wasn't looking to work forty hours a week since my kids were so young. I wanted to earn a little extra money while doing something I loved. I wanted to make enough to be able to stay home with the kids."

By taking the time to really plan and evaluate her idea of a mom-friendly coffee shop, Mandy realized it didn't fit with what she wanted out of a business and was able to avoid lots of pitfalls down the road. There are some who will tell you to "just do it." We think it's better to look before you leap.

Bring your idea to the people you trust

So you think you're on to something? Now it's time to go to your people. Ask a group of trusted friends, family, and colleagues what they think of your ideas—these are the people who know you best. But remember that you're not just looking for pats on the back—people who will tell you that any idea you have is a great one and that they're sure "you'll be successful at whatever you put your mind to, dear." No. Ask the people in your life for their *honest* opinions. And remember, you haven't done anything yet, so you can afford to listen to their suggestions.

You'll get the biggest bang for your buck if you consult with people who know something about the industry you're contemplating entering, in addition to knowing you personally. Samantha Linton—remember, the erotica videographer?—found an effective solution. She says, "I have two mentors who are both in the television industry. But more than just knowing the industry, they know *me*."

It doesn't need to be rocket science. Our two families have had a regular dinner together for the past twenty years. For months we asked our Sunday Night Dinner group for feedback on our ideas. Sometimes the people who know and love you have more insights about your strengths and weaknesses than you do.

Assessing the viability of a business

Now that you've landed on an idea, it's time to ask yourself some real questions. We've seen some pretty silly businesses in our time, which led us to create a little saying that goes, "Just because it's an idea doesn't mean it's a business-worthy idea." We're sure you can think of companies in your community that make you scratch your head. In our neighbourhood, there was a retail store that sold water. That's right. It was a water store. They sold bottled water of all different varieties. We can't imagine what they were thinking. Not only is buying water in disposable bottles very out of vogue, but more importantly, water is *free*. Talk about a tough business model. Needless to say, the water shop is no longer around.

IS OPPORTUNITY KNOCKING?

There are lots of terrific business ideas out there, but not all of them are true business *opportunities*. An opportunity is an idea for a product or service that customers actually want to buy, that you can make and sell profitably, that you can make and sell better than your competitors, and that you enjoy making and selling.

—Prof. Reuber

Know your customer

Who will your customer be? Ours is Tracy. No kidding. We just happen to have a disproportionate number of customers in our database named Tracy. Prototypically, Tracy is a thirty-something mom of a young child who lives in or near a large urban centre. Everyone she knows is pregnant so she has lots of baby gifts to buy. She shops online because it's convenient. She wants to buy a baby gift that's special, but also practical—no cashmere baby blankets for this gal. That's our girl—Tracy.

Now, we didn't always know who our customer would be, but we found by making certain decisions about the price of our blankets and how we sell them, a certain type of customer has emerged. We think about Tracy every time we consider a change to pricing, design, or marketing activities. (The fact that Tracy is basically *us* makes this easier than it might be if we were selling to an entirely different customer.)

Ask yourself who the end-user of your product or service will be, and why they will buy it. If there is a strong reason for them to buy it—if they get value from buying it—then you have a compelling *value proposition*. Having a compelling value proposition is one characteristic that makes an idea an opportunity. Remember Victoria Turner on the airplane with the sling? It was pretty clear that people were interested in the product.

Know your market

Once you've got a sense of your customer and just what you can do for them, you're on your way to figuring out the market for your product or service and, most importantly, how you are going to make money. In other words, you're thinking about the economics of your business. Having good economics is a second characteristic that makes an idea an opportunity. We'll talk more about this later, but in short, you want your sales revenue to be high and steady. But don't take it from us, take it from Rebecca. The three questions below are key considerations at this stage, according to the expert.

WHAT IS THE SIZE OF THE MARKET FOR YOUR BUSINESS?

Ask yourself: How many potential customers are there now and how many will there be two years from now? This tells you the market size and growth.

Because: Your sales will be higher when there are more people out there who are motivated to buy your product or service. And it's even better when you expect this number to increase.

Ask yourself: How long will your customer be with you? We all wish the answer would be "forever," but each customer has a life cycle.

Because: Acquiring a customer is usually more expensive than keeping one. You are likely to have a steadier revenue stream if you have recurring sales (think toner cartridges in your printer), and for a longer period of time, than if customers buy your product just once.

Ask yourself: How long does it take a customer to decide to buy your product or service? Each type of customer has a sales cycle.

Because: The more expensive or complex your product is, the longer it will take someone to decide to buy it. If you're selling a service to a business or government, it could take quite a while. During this period, you will be spending money to make the sale but won't get revenue back until (unless) the sale is made.

—Prof. Reuber

Know your rivals

You should also think about your competitors. Is anyone else doing this? Why or why not? Can you do it better? We recently chatted with a mom of two young children who is thinking about starting a home organization business. We thought it was a pretty nifty idea: she's super-organized and could work part-time to accommodate the needs of her kids. When we referred her to a woman we know who offers a similar service, she was stunned. She thought that she had invented the idea and had *no clue* that there even *were* other people out there who are home organizers—let alone someone in our direct network. Gals, we're begging you, do your homework. Get Googling! The Internet actually makes it pretty easy. Everything you need to know is literally at your fingertips.

In addition to your direct competitors (companies that offer the same product or service in the same market as you), you'll want to consider your indirect competitors (companies that offer a similar product or service, or perhaps the same product or service but marketed in a different way). For example, if you want to open a cupcake shop, you'll certainly want to know what other cupcake shops are in your area—but don't forget about the nearby bakery that specializes in children's birthday cakes, or the supermarket across the street that sells cupcakes too.

But it's not just current competitors you need to think about. Let's say you have a compelling value proposition, strong economics, and no one else is selling a product like yours. Customers want to buy from you and your sales are going to be great. What happens next? Sadly, another entrepreneur will see you making money and decide to start a similar business. Or, an existing business will decide that they can widen their product line to sell a product just like yours. So, even if you can't find any current competitors, you need to think about what makes your product or service unique and how you can keep your competitors—current and future—at bay.

In our case, we did not *invent* the personalized baby blanket. But we did think about how we could do it differently (or better or faster or cheaper, etc.), and it's allowed us to sleep easily at night. For instance, when we looked around and saw that many personalized blankets were embroidered, we decided to use bold appliquéd lettering. We also decided that we would only create original designs that we were proud to sell. We felt that our product was different, but we also wanted to compete on customer service. Back when our competitors were just taking orders by telephone, we had a fully functioning e-commerce website. We wanted to make it as easy as possible for our customers to order from us. And we've always treated our customers just the way we'd like to be treated ourselves.

HOW DO YOU COMPARE TO THE COMPETITION?

One way to start thinking about your distinctiveness among competitors is to compare your product or service with others on the market in terms of its characteristics. This is called your position in the market. Focus on two characteristics that matter most to your customers. Going back to the cupcake shop example, your customers might value most your use of organic ingredients and your large variety of flavours. Or they might care most about your low prices and the fact that they can buy your cupcakes in convenience stores. These are two different positions in the market. When you are communicating the benefits of your product to your customers, you are positioning it with respect to the most valued characteristics. Don't be alarmed if you are not sure at the start what positioning is best in terms of attracting the types of customers you want. You may need to experiment to learn more about what characteristics matter most to them.

—Prof. Reuber

The point is that you can deliver a product or service that is distinctive from your competitors in ways that your customers value. This is the third characteristic that makes an idea an opportunity.

Know yourself—does this idea turn your crank?

Okay, you've found an idea that is truly an opportunity from a business perspective. But is it an opportunity for *you*?

A friend recently mentioned that there is a real need for a bagel place in her neighbourhood and she's thinking about opening up shop. "Great!" we said. "Can you imagine yourself working behind the counter in a bagel store?" (She couldn't.) Then we asked her, "Would you be willing to work behind the counter of an existing bagel store to learn what it's all about?" (She wouldn't.) So, no matter how much an idea makes sense from a business perspective, if you're not into it, it's going to be pretty unpleasant to tough out the hard times. Do yourself a favour and ask yourself if this idea is for you.

6

Care to join me?

Partnership for mompreneurs

*"A friendship founded on business is a good deal better
than a business founded on friendship."*
—*John D. Rockefeller*

"Hooey! Rockefeller didn't know mompreneurs like us."
—*Amy and Danielle*

When you think that you'd like to start your own business, deciding
who to do it with—or without—is a pretty big deal. For many
women, deciding whether or not to take on a partner is at the
heart of their decision about how to move forward with their
business.

Just to complicate things, "partnership" is actually a legal term
that refers to a business entity in which the partners—or owners—
share in the profits or losses of the business. This is not the same
thing as a sole proprietorship or corporation, which have different
tax and liability implications. There are lots of resources to explain
the differences among a partnership, sole proprietorship, and corporation, and your accountant will be able to clear up which option
is most appropriate for you. What we're talking about here is not

necessarily a "legal" partnership (although it might be), but the choice of working with another human being versus going it alone.

If starting your own business is like giving birth to a baby (oh, and it is), then taking on a business partner is most definitely like getting married. Like in marriage, there are many reasons business partners might be attracted to one another. And just like in marriage, partnership has plenty of ups and downs. Let's start with what common wisdom tells us about partnerships.

One advantage of a partnership is that you'll share whatever costs you incur to start up. You'll also have someone to share the load. All the work and responsibility of starting a new business can be divided between you and your partner. And in partnership, having differences between partners is widely considered to be a good thing. If your partner has a different background from you, has different skills, and knows different people, you both ought to be able to accomplish more than if you were each flying solo. Finally, partnership can provide support and motivation. Waking up day in and day out, getting the kids out the door, and then putting your head down to get to work can be a tough slog. We don't know how the solo-preneurs do it!

And then there are the arguments against partnership. One strike against partnership is liability. Each partner is on the hook for the actions of the other. So if your mommy friend goes off the deep end—and we know of a case where this happened—you will be responsible for all of your business's debt—not just your part of it. Another potentially negative argument against partnership is shared profitability. You'll keep what you reap, but you'll have to split it with your partner. In other words, your business will have to make twice as much to feed two mouths. Then there are the softer arguments against partnership, like what happens when you and your partner don't share the same vision, opinions, work ethic, decisions, or goals. Since you alone do not control your business, you and your partner need to be on the same page. If not, and we've seen it lots of times, one of two things happens: the business dissolves or the partnership breaks up. And if you and your partner are friends, your friendship may not survive either.

We're going on the record right now to say that we are HUGE fans of partnership for mompreneurs. Juggling a business and a family *is not the same* as starting a business when there are no kids in the picture. As such, the old standards about partnership just don't account for the unique circumstances in which a mompreneur might find herself.

How to find what you're looking for

When you're looking at your personal criteria for starting your business, you'll want to ask yourself if you need to consider a partner—for either personal or financial reasons. If you're launching a service business based on your professional past, partnership may not be relevant because you can go it alone. Or, if you've come up with a brilliant idea and are confident to go out and execute it, then you're good to go.

NO DUMPING
Even if you just don't want or need a partner, you will still need a sounding board. You WILL need someone you can talk to about your business. You can form an advisory board, seek out a mentor, join a networking group, or hire a business coach. Just find an outlet! DO NOT dump all your issues on your husband or best friend.

But let's say that you are interested in teaming up. What should you look for in a partner? We've come up with a bunch of things every mompreneur will want to consider when looking for her business partner.

Are your goals in sync?

If you've gone through the exercise of deciding what you want to get out of your business, then you've articulated your goals—to yourself. If you plan on taking on a partner, you need to be able to spell it out to her as well.

The co-founders of SavvyMom.ca set out their goals for their business—and their partnership—from the start. Sarah Morgenstern and Minnow Hamilton say, "We had a partnership agreement from the get-go. We formalized our arrangement despite a lot of trust and friendship between us. It was sort of like a pre-nup—we didn't want to sacrifice our friendship for the business. We professionalized our friendship."

Debbie Zinman is a co-founder of EchoAge, a charity-driven, online birthday party service. Of her partnership with fellow mom Alison Smith she says, "We share values. What binds us is our shared vision for the business."

One mompreneur we know was in a partnership with another mom who did not share her goals. Here's what happened when she was in that boat: "We worked together for several years. As we grew, the needs of the business changed and inequities in our partnership became apparent. I realized that we had different goals in mind for the business and our lifestyles. We parted ways and it was difficult. It was a business decision but it was taken personally by people around her."

If your goals don't match up, the partnership won't last. Spend the time up front to make sure you're on the same page.

THE TIES THAT BIND

No matter how well you know and like your prospective future business partner, a legal partnership agreement is essential. It will protect you both from anything unforeseen, and can spare you a lot of expense and difficulty down the road.

—Prof. Reuber

What does each of you bring to the table?

Ideally you'll find a partner whose skills are complementary to your own. This way, you've got a broader base of knowledge and expertise than if you're going it alone. (This was not the case for us. In fact, our resumes couldn't be more similar—same universities, same degrees, even hired by the same management consulting firm. We could not possess a more similar skill set. To mitigate this, we've found points of differentiation between us that make dividing our roles quite natural.) In a perfect world, your business partner will be strong where you are not. The idea is for the whole to be greater than the sum of the parts.

Do you want to be on the ride with this person?

Bottom line: you can't work with someone you just plain don't get along with. You *can* work with someone you don't really jive with, but it might not be much fun. We love how this mompreneur explained it: "This business would never have gotten off the ground if not for my partner. I'm good on ideas, but I wouldn't have executed. She is the opposite. She is really driven, frugal— great qualities that complement mine. The downside is that I don't always like hanging out with her."

Running a business *is* work and not one long coffee date. You need to be able to communicate with your partner about business issues. Business coach Paula Jubinville says, "Partnership can be a lovely thing. You both have to be healthy people—you have to be able to take criticism from one another." You'll want a partner who will listen to you on the one hand, but will have the conviction to bring her own ideas to the table too. You may not be hiring a new BFF, but it is best to find someone you can be yourself around.

Who's got what?

Nobody enjoys talking about money, and we're no exception. Heck, women talk about their sex lives more freely than they'll chat about the family finances. Nonetheless, when checking out someone as a potential partner, her financial situation might be relevant. If your partner is a trust-fund baby, her business aspirations might well be different from your own. Conversely, if your partner wants to replace her former professional income, but you're just looking to earn some pocket change, that too will affect how you approach the business. Make sure your partner's financial needs and goals are in line with your own.

That's it. We'd say more on the topic of personal finances but we're feeling uncomfortable already.

What does her present—and future—look like?

Where's your partner at in her personal life? Is she married? Is she a mom? Things are bound to go more smoothly if you're both at the same life stage. It's going to be easier for your partner to be flexible when your Junior's got a cold if her Junior had a cold last week! What kinds of commitments does she have outside of work? Life is full of unexpected bumps in the road—will you be able to handle it if something pulls her away from the business for a time? Or if her life is on a different course than your own? There's no right answer here—just cause for pause.

Maybe you'll lead largely separate lives, or maybe you'll come to lean on your partner heavily. During a particularly rough patch in her personal life, Eryn Green of Sweetpea Baby Food and Organic Snacks heavily relied on her partner, Tamar Wagman. She says, "If I didn't have a partner, I probably would have given up on the business."

And sometimes your personal lives come to a head. One mompreneur tells us a difficult story: "Looking for some companionship in my business, I brought in a partner. She had a business background, was very creative, and had tons of energy. For a time, everything was good—and then my partner got sick. She was pretty much absent from the business for months. I was totally overwhelmed and trying to keep it all afloat. Even though I knew she was sick I was angry because I wanted her to step down—I didn't want to be put in the position of asking her to. Over some difficult conversations she backed out of the business."

While it's hard to predict what will happen in your partnership, doing your homework is worth it. Just like when you get married, it's better to talk about the Big Issues before you put the rings on each other's fingers.

FOUR QUESTIONS TO ASK YOURSELF ABOUT PARTNERSHIP

1. **Do I really want a partner?** Having a partner has clear advantages but it also means giving up some control over the direction and day-to-day operations of the business. Make sure you know that you want an equal partner to share in the decisions, and not just someone to help you out with your financing needs or your workload. If that's what you want, you should be looking for an investor or an employee, but not a business partner.

If you answer yes to this question and have a possible partner in mind, then you should ask yourself the next three questions.

2. **Do we share a vision for this business?** Are we emphasizing high growth or are we building a small but stable company? You will regularly be making decisions that affect the trajectory of your business. For example, do we invest in developing a client who is likely to pay off in a big way, but not for a year? Do we take a pay cut so we can invest in new product development? Do we go after a potentially lucrative Asian market that requires a great deal of travel? Do we try to sell in the big box stores, which could increase our production requirements and squeeze our margins but offer us access to a huge market? To answer questions like these, you and your partner need to agree on ultimate objectives so you trust each other's judgment.

3. **Can we work together on a day-to-day basis?** You're going to be spending a lot of time with your partner, so you need to be sure that you like and respect her, and trust her integrity and competence. Dividing up the tasks is easier if you enjoy doing different things. Also, it can be helpful if you're at the same stage in your personal lives. A partner with small children is more likely to understand that you want to attend your daughter's soccer game.

4. **Does this person bring important resources to the business?** You will be sharing business risks and rewards, so it's important that you both bring something valuable to the table. Ideally, you will be able to find a partner who has skills and business contacts in areas where you lack them.

—Prof. Reuber

It sounds like finding a business partner is a tall order—and it can be. Mompreneur Elisa Palter of *Help! We've Got Kids* says it well: "Don't let the fact that this person is your friend lead to assumptions that what she has is what you need in a partner. You need to look at all of this person's skills and abilities. (Is she a salesperson? Is she risk-averse or a risk taker?) It's all very nice when you spend time at the park with your friend and her baby. Things are fun at the park. There are no financial worries at the park. But your friend isn't as much fun when she can't make a sales call. Or read a financial statement. You need to look at the personality and skills you require—not just as a friend. My partner and I say that we interviewed each other and we hired each other."

Partnership: Our story

When we were developing our own entrepreneurship criteria, being in business together was right up at the top of the list. We just knew that whatever we did, we wanted to do it together. We can each say that there is no way we would have started this business on our own. (And there certainly is no way that either one of us could *run* the business on our own today.)

We were not cavalier about the idea of partnership. On the contrary, we went out and "interviewed" all the business partners we could find. We asked about their skills sets, how they divided their responsibilities, and what they did when they disagreed. We wanted to be aware of all the potential pitfalls before we signed up.

We have no reason not to be honest here. Everyone we spoke to told us not to do it. As the best of friends, no one we knew wanted to see us risk our friendship. So what would cause us to ignore the thoughtful advice of friends and colleagues? We knew our friendship would be okay no matter what (we're more sisters than friends, and our friendship has a solid track record). But more importantly, we chose partnership because we wanted to have babies!

Despite hearing that a key to our success would be a clear division of roles, we did the exact opposite. In the early days of the business (for a solid year, in fact) we did not divide our jobs at all. We divided *tasks* if it made sense, but we certainly did not have job descriptions. Why did we do it this way? We knew that a time would come in the not-too-distant future wherein one of us would have to hand off the business *entirely* to the other one after having a child. So it was pretty important that we both knew the ropes.

We think partnership is a great way to mitigate the demands of your business when you've got a small child in tow. Knowing that there is someone you trust to steward the business in your absence is a huge deal. Now, you'll have to be up front with your partner about exactly what kind of maternity leave you have in mind. You're best off to consult with your business partner well in advance in order to manage everyone's expectations.

TEN THINGS A PARTNER CAN DO FOR YOU

1. She can assume a portion of the financial risk, helping you make the entrepreneurial jump.
2. She can celebrate your successes with you.
3. She can commiserate with you when things don't go as planned.
4. She can cover for you when your kids need you.
5. She can make you accountable for getting work done.
6. She can allow you to pass off uncomfortable situations by being the "bad cop" with customers and suppliers.
7. She can help you avoid strain on your marriage and other relationships by giving you a forum to talk about the business.
8. She can take a turn being the cheerleader for the business when you're finding it a slog.
9. She can let you take a maternity leave or vacation without worrying about the business.

10. She can teach you how to truly work at a relationship and not let stresses build up.

All right. We know you're thinking that it all sounds too good to be true. Are you wondering if we fight? Of course we do. In the beginning it was hard sometimes learning how to work together. Before we became business partners we could let the little things that crop up in any relationship (a misunderstood word, a tense moment) go, with the knowledge that it would have passed by the next time we spoke to or saw each other. But here's the thing—there is simply no place to hide in a business partnership, especially if you're locked up in an office together all day.

Over time we've learned to address every issue as it arises. We cannot afford to let any tension build up—either in the business or in the friendship. There's too much crossover. We have a perfect track record of not going to bed mad (which is considerably better than the track records we have in our marriages!). This can mean late-night phone calls to resolve whatever has come up. We do our best to communicate with each other as friends and business partners—and have found that the hot button issues now come up less frequently and are dealt with more easily than in the infancy of our business. But thinking that you can have a conflict-free partnership is about as realistic as thinking you're never going to fight with your husband.

The unexpected partner

When speaking to mompreneurs across North America, we began to develop a theory on partnership. In general, the mompreneurs with business partners tend not to involve their husbands in their businesses in any significant way. This definitely holds true for us.

Our husbands have little interest in when we place the thread order, have fabric delivered, or if a customer is pissy. We don't blame them. They have their own jobs to contend with. The good news is that, as business partners, we can talk about all the minute details of our business with one another until we're blue in the face. Tricia Mumby of Mabel's Labels says she doesn't talk about work to anyone else— including her husband. She says since the four partners talk about work so much between them, they don't even want to talk about it at the end of the day.

But what if you don't have a business partner? Well, there *are* a lot of little details and there are a lot of decisions to be made on a daily basis, and sometimes doing it entirely on your own can be tough. It's our observation that mompreneurs without business partners tend to involve their husbands in their businesses to a greater degree. We've met mompreneurs—solo operators—whose husbands help them set up at trade shows, order supplies for them, or do their deliveries.

We've also met mompreneurs who consider their husbands their business partners. Candace Alper is the mom of a seven-year-old girl and owner of Name Your Tune Inc., which makes personalized children's music CDs. Candace says, "My husband has always been my business partner. I run things by him and we make decisions together, but ultimately he will defer to me." Candace's husband has a full-fledged career of his own, but she uses him as her sounding board. Several years into her business, Candace brought in her best friend since nursery school, Jessica Kaplan, as a partner. Both Jessica's and Candace's husbands are now actively involved in the business.

We've also met mompreneurs who have become so successful that their husbands left their professions to become partners in their wives' companies. Michelle Wright of Wrightway Premium Incentives is an example of a husband-joins-wife team. She says, "My promotional products business was really important to me.

But when my daughter was born, she became my priority. My husband really hated his job, so we decided to just plunk him in the business. He had to learn everything. We're different—I'm the ideas person, and he's a natural salesman, which is great, because I'm not. Now, my priority is the kids and the house. We fight, but it's not bad because this is for our family."

So who knows, your future partner just might be the person you sleep next to!

Or maybe another member of the family will join you in your business. After all, it makes perfect sense to work with someone with whom you already have a trusting relationship. Joanne Schneeweiss, mom and founder of KidsAroundCanada.com, ended up with a partner she didn't plan for—her father. She says: "I own my corporation, but for all intents and purposes, my father has become my business partner. I never would have predicted this, but his career wound down just as I decided to turn my hobby into a business. He helped me do this with his extensive business background. Now I manage the website and marketing and he does all the back-end administration. I bounce ideas off him. What if he hadn't become part of my business? I don't think I would have continued with it. I have a very good relationship with him. There is trust."

While our partnership is key to our business and our sanity, we also appreciate that you may not have your best friend of twenty years available to you for your business venture. And we would no more recommend jumping into an iffy partnership any more than we would suggest you marry Mr. Wrong. If the right partner for you isn't available, don't fret. While we think partnership is ideal for mompreneurs, we have every confidence that you can do this on your own.

7

Looking at the big picture

Where do you want this business to go?

When you're thinking about starting your own business, you'll want to chart the course you think your business will take. People call this "planning from 30,000 feet." (You get a great view and can usually avoid the motion sickness.) Ask yourself what your long-term plan for your business is. What do you hope is the final destination for this project? And don't tell us you just can't imagine it. We can't imagine raising teenagers either, but we know we'll want them to leave the house at some point!

This process is like signing a prenuptial agreement before you get married. It seems crazy to think about the end of something before you've even gotten started, but it forces you to think of all the potential eventualities. Of course you can't predict everything that will happen between now and the point when you no longer work in your business, but you can think about what you hope will happen.

In our case, we wanted to grow Admiral Road modestly and work part-time until our kids were on their way (which meant being in school full-time), and then we wanted it to morph into something bigger and more full-time. Maybe you want to run a nice business until your kids are in school full-time, at which point you'll return to your former career. Maybe you want to grow a business to a point where it's large enough to sell it. Maybe you want to see your company listed on the stock exchange one day. And maybe you want to work in your business until the day you die. Here's our common refrain again: it doesn't matter what the plan is, just make sure you're clear on it.

Trish Magwood is an author, spokesperson, and television host who ran a successful cooking studio for ten years before selling it. She puts it this way: "You need to know how you're going to get out before you get in. You can easily become so entrenched in the business that you lose sight of the big picture." Of course it's going to change along the way—it would be downright boring if it didn't. But having a roadmap of where you're going certainly isn't going to hurt.

While you're thinking about how long you're in this for and what your exit plan is, you need to consider the possibility that you will change along with your business. Here's something we learned along the way: even if you don't start out as a natural entrepreneur, you'll likely turn into one. It goes like this: you get incredibly inspired and work like mad on a great idea. You're excited at the ways you can grow and everything is stimulating. Over time you build your customer base and perfect your product or service. And then something interesting happens—you're just running your business.

Let's say you have a great idea for a specialty clothing store. You need to source vendors, find and outfit a space, develop your brand and packaging, and market yourself. It's incredibly stimulating despite the hard work. Then let's say you find yourself a few years in, well-established with a loyal clientele. One day you will likely look up and realize that you are in the business of managing a retail store. You will be concerned with operations, customer service, financial management, etc. You may tackle new marketing initiatives, new products, and so on, but you'll be very actively involved in the operational side of the business.

In our case, we worked like crazy for the first five years to grow our business to a certain critical mass and we worked the kinks out of our systems. Then we looked up one day and realized we worked in a mail-order company. We love our business, but somehow it wasn't feeding our creative energy in the way it had earlier on. That's when we started working on new projects. Today we still spend time on the operations of Admiral Road, but we've also found other ways to nurture our inner entrepreneurs.

Running an established business is still stimulating and hard work, but it's no longer the same start-up rush. You could probably compare it to the infatuation of a budding romance versus the comfortable love of a decades-long marriage. Trish Magwood puts it this way, "I thought being an entrepreneur meant creative freedom and flexibility, but as a business owner you put yourself in shackles from Day One."

We don't think that the "shackles" of running your business have to hurt necessarily, but there are day-to-day realities. The only problem with this scenario is that you may well have become a "serial entrepreneur" at some point along the way. The thrill of starting up can be pretty addictive, so make sure you're getting into a business you want to be in for the long term, or have a good plan for how to commit your serial acts of entrepreneurship.

Once you go through the exercises we've outlined here, from idea generation to analysis and evaluation, it's time to move on. Get out your notebook and let's get planning.

PART 3

GESTATION:
THE IMPORTANCE OF BUSINESS PLANNING

*So you've decided to start your own business and you've
figured out what kind of business to be in. You're well on
your way. In our terms, you've planned for this "baby" and
even gotten yourself knocked up. Now you've got what we call
the gestation period in front of you. Much as your baby takes
some time to develop all of the necessary functions of life, so
does your business. Your pregnancy brings nausea, fatigue,
endless trips to the washroom, back pain, heartburn, and
so much more, right? Well, you'll have a few hurdles to
get over as your business baby gets ready for birth
as well. Just like you wouldn't want to deliver your
real-life baby before it's fully "cooked," you
want to make sure your business is ready to
go before you hang out your shingle.*

8

A blueprint for your biz

Writing your business plan

One of the grandmas in our lives has a saying that we've adopted as our own mantra: "Start as you intend to finish." We try to apply this in our parenting as well as in our business. If you want the world to view your company as a serious endeavour, taking the time to write your business plan is a great place to start.

FAMOUS WORDS

Those who plan do better than those who do not plan even though they rarely stick to their plan.

—Winston Churchill

Many of the mompreneurs we spoke to never wrote formal business plans. And several even expressed disdain for them. Nicole Morell, owner of Honey-bunch.com, an online children's toy, gift, and party supply shop weighed in: "Business plans are ridiculous! How can you know what your sales will be? The only reason I wrote a business plan was to take it to the bank when I needed to finance the start-up of my store. I had no idea what the banker wanted to see. 'Does $150,000 in sales sound good?' I asked her. She shrugged her shoulders and said that she didn't know either."

Nicole's reaction was hardly atypical. She wasn't the only person to scoff at a business plan. Some mompreneurs told us that they thought it was "limiting" to write a business plan.

Martha Scully of Canadian Sitter is a former infant therapist and mom of two who owns multiple job-posting websites. When it came for her initial planning, she got resourceful. Martha says, "I didn't write a business plan. However, I did make use of the free hour of a marketing professional, accountant, and lawyer offered up by my local community. Many communities offer this and it's very helpful." You can visit our website www.mominc.ca for a list of resources to assist mompreneurs with business planning.

That being said, we're pretty sold on doing a business plan. We think it's really important and strongly recommend you take the time to do it. We'll even show you how. But first, why bother? Most entrepreneurs who write a business plan do so because they need to borrow money from a bank or investor.

A RESUMÉ FOR YOUR BUSINESS
Lenders expect you to have a business plan just like a recruiter expects you to have a resumé when you're applying for a job.

—Prof. Reuber

But we think the most important beneficiary of your business plan is YOU. A business plan is intended to demonstrate how your company will make money and provide returns on the initial investment. It's an exercise in laying out the potential for profit and risk of your business venture, and for looking at the ways you're uniquely positioned to win at the game of business.

People are often enamoured with one aspect of their new business, and can neglect other important aspects. For example, some entrepreneurs spend a lot of time and effort developing the perfect product, but don't think enough about how they're going to get it to their customers. Others may understand their competition cold, but haven't spent enough time checking out possible suppliers and how much lead time they need. Writing a business plan forces you to look at your business from all angles.

—Prof. Reuber

If you need to borrow money, a business plan is essential, but doesn't it sound like a pretty worthwhile use of a few days even if you're only investing your own cash? If nothing else, a business plan will help you articulate your own language about your business.

Alison Kramer, a former social worker, spent the time to write a business plan for her nursing bra company, Nummies. She says, "I did a business plan even though I didn't need to borrow money— it's critical no matter what. It's a good exercise—it's a good hard look at why you're doing it. It's a real business, not just an idea. You have to look at competitors, risk, etc."

Given our strong feelings on the subject it should come as no surprise that we wrote a formal business plan. We took it to the bank when we started our business. Although we used our own cash to start the business, we knew we'd likely need financing down the road and wanted to be positioned to get it. We also needed to set up merchant accounts to accept credit cards and to negotiate the best service plans and terms for all of our banking activities.

TIP: BANK ON IT

Choose your bank carefully. Call them up and ask what they can do for your new business. There can be quite a bit of difference among banks in terms of rates and services available to new businesses.

We looked at the five major banks where we live and found the bank that most wanted to do business with us. Then we set up a meeting with the person who would be responsible for our account. That was on a Friday and we were scheduled to meet our banker on Monday. We spent the weekend banging out our business plan. (It's really not that hard, we promise.)

When we went into that meeting, we can tell you that our banker was delighted to see us and our neat business plan. Think about it—most small businesses fall into the category we like to refer to as "Joe's Pet Grooming and Coffee Shop." Most small-business owners are technicians in their field (barbers, dry cleaners, bakers, etc.) and are not necessarily business savvy. You have to imagine that bankers see figures on the backs of napkins or worse. Our banker looked positively relieved to see that we had thought about our business.

After a brief meeting and a look through our plan, he turned to the woman responsible for actually opening the accounts and said, "Give them whatever they want." This is a true story. It taught us the value of being prepared and putting our best foot forward in any situation.

TIP: SCHEDULE TIME TO CREATE A BUSINESS PLAN

If you find it hard to carve out time to write your business plan, try giving yourself a schedule. Set aside one night a week for eight weeks. Let the family know you aren't available, lock yourself up with your computer, and you'll be amazed at what you can get done.

Not only did our business plan help us make nice with our banker, it had lots of other benefits as well. We pulled the marketing plan out, stuck it on the wall of our basement office, and followed it for the rest of the year. And we thought about our numbers in terms of the financial projections in our business plan for the first several years. (We were off the mark in those projections, but that's another story we'll get to later.) Even if you don't use your plan right away, it's one of those things that doesn't go bad—it'll need to be updated as you go, of course, but it's a terrifically valuable tool.

Writing your business plan

We hope we've now convinced you to take the time to do a business plan. So what exactly does writing one involve? It's just a collection of documents outlining the various aspects of your business. Here's a little about each aspect of a business plan. You can refer to our website www.mominc.ca to see some samples.

Executive summary

Your executive summary is sort of the Cole's Notes (remember those?) of your business plan. It should provide a one- to two-page (no longer) overview of the rest of the sections in your plan. Write a few sentences about what your company sells, the market and your customer, how you will make and sell your product or service, your management team, and your financial projections. Even though the executive summary is the first thing the reader will see, it makes sense to write it last since you'll already have your language and key messages in place by then.

MAKE A GOOD IMPRESSION
How important is your executive summary? If you're writing your business plan only for yourself, it isn't that important, because you know what's in it. But, if want your plan to entice a potential banker, investor, partner, or

employee to become involved in your business, the executive summary is the most important section because it will determine whether people will go on to read the rest of the plan. If they think that your business concept is too confusing, too boring, or too unrealistic, then they are unlikely to read further. You've lost their confidence.

—Prof. Reuber

Company description

Here you'll be giving the reader a sense of your company. Where are you located? What do you sell? To whom? How many of you are working in the business and what do you bring to the table professionally?

THE BENEFITS OF INCORPORATION

Most new firms in North America are incorporated, although it is also possible to start a business as a sole proprietorship or as a partnership. The advantage of incorporation is that the business is a legal entity in itself—separate from the owners—that can enter into contracts, own property, pay taxes, sue and be sued, and be sold or inherited. It usually isn't difficult, time-consuming, or expensive to incorporate, but the requirements and the process vary among different countries, states, and provinces. Most governments maintain a website that tells people what paperwork is required to start a business (incorporate, get a tax number, register a business name, etc.) in their jurisdiction.

—Prof. Reuber

Industry analysis

This section looks at the overall industry you'll be working in. Let's say you are opening an online shoe store. You would include some information and statistics about shoe sales overall (e.g., The U.S. shoe store industry includes about 30,000 stores with combined annual revenue of almost $25 billion). You'll want to mention any significant trends in the industry (e.g., In 2009, online shoe sales reached $3 billion—a figure expected to double by 2014). You'll also want to identify your key competitors and where you would fit in (e.g., Although key competitors such as Zappos have a large market share, there is still considerable room for more specialized companies like [your new company name].).

The industry analysis section is especially important if you're entering a relatively new industry. When Eryn Green and Tamar Wagman started Sweetpea Baby Food and Organic Snacks they were entering a brand new category—there were virtually no other providers of frozen organic baby food at the time they came to market. It was especially important for them to demonstrate that there was room in the baby food industry for their new category.

How do you find this information? Start online and see what you can turn up. (The stats we included above about the online shoe industry are fictional, but we were able to find the actual information online in about three minutes.) Then dig further. There are plenty of government resources to be found online. Also, most industries have professional associations that publish statistics on their field. The SupperWorks mompreneurs, for example, relied heavily on the Easy Meal Prep Association when they were starting up their business. The association provided all kinds of useful information and support, not just for business planning purposes but for practical start-up info as well.

Still stumped? Look for trade shows in your specific industry and call up the organizers to see what info they have. You can also call sales reps, stores, etc., to see what info they can give you. If you're polite and honest about what you're looking for, you'll find that many people will be quite helpful.

Market analysis

Here you'll talk about the specific market you'll be competing in. If you want to open a daycare centre in Toledo, you would talk about the population of Toledo and how many children are born in the city each year. You would also talk about the key demographics in your specific area to demonstrate that your pricing will be appropriate for the market you are operating in.

Here is an example (with hypothetical statistics): "In the Old Orchard neighbourhood, the average household income is $60,000 and the average education of the household is undergraduate university. Each household has an average of 1.7 children under the age of six."

You would want to mention how many other daycare options exist for the population you want to serve and identify the excess demand (waiting lists for existing centres, etc.). You would then conclude that there is a demand for your daycare centre in Old Orchard, as well as a population with the means to pay for your childcare services.

If you're opening up a location-specific business, you can easily find population and demographic facts from the city, province, or state in which you want to work. Look through the phone book or online directory to see what other companies are working in the same sector as you.

Competitive analysis

In this section, you'll identify who your competitors are and then show why you have a competitive edge. This exercise is extremely valuable. It will not only make you aware of who else is out there competing with you for the same dollars, but it will force you to look at the strengths and weaknesses of those businesses.

Let's return to the daycare centre example. Imagine that there are already two established daycares in the area in which you want to open. Assume both have excellent reputations and a loyal following. Maybe you can offer longer hours of care to parents. Maybe you have a better location or a specialized curriculum. Perhaps you're going to invest in camera technology so anxious parents can watch their children remotely via webcam. Knowing what the other guy (or gal) has that you don't can force you to find your competitive edge. If there is one thing we've learned from our conversations with mompreneurs, it's that your competitors can take up an obscene amount of mental space—so know who you're dealing with from the get-go.

CALL IN THE SWOT TEAM

SWOT is an acronym that stands for strengths, weaknesses, opportunities, and threats. A SWOT analysis is a great tool to analyze your business venture. Identifying the strengths and weaknesses of your company provides an internal assessment, while identifying its opportunities and threats provides an external assessment. Thinking about all four aspects of your business together will help you to find a strategy that matches your company's capabilities with the realities of your environment.

Strengths: These are things that you and your company are good at compared with your competition. Strengths can include things like a respected brand, a strong cash flow position, inexpensive production facilities, a loyal customer base, a well-placed mentor in the business community, a great location, great marketing skills, and proven technology.

Weaknesses: These are things that you and your company are not so good at compared with your competition. Weaknesses can include things like a weak distribution network, high operating costs, lack of marketing expertise, a ho-hum product that isn't getting traction in the market, and product-quality issues.

Opportunities: These are conditions in the market that are favourable for your company. Opportunities can include things like demand for your product in new markets, demand for related products, advantageous changes in regulations or trade barriers, and changes in customers' buying patterns.

Threats: These are conditions in the market that are unfavourable for your company. Threats can include things like the emergence of a new competitor, an economic slowdown that affects your customers' willingness to buy, adverse changes in regulations and trade barriers, increased costs, and reduced demand for your product.

Once you have identified your strengths, weaknesses, opportunities, and threats, you can develop a strategy by thinking about the following questions:
- What opportunities do we have the strengths to pursue with a high likelihood of success?
- What threats are we most vulnerable to, and how can we develop strengths to defend against them?
- Which weaknesses are holding us back, and how can we reverse them?
- Which strengths are most valuable in allowing us to keep the competition at bay, and how can we stay strong in these areas?

—Prof. Reuber

Sales and marketing activities

Sales: There are different sales channels for different kinds of businesses, so how you sell your product will depend on the kind of business you set up. In your business plan, explain which business model you have chosen. If you plan to sell your product directly to the end-user, then this is a business-to-consumer model (like Admiral Road). If you plan to sell your product directly to other companies, then you have a business-to-business model (like Sweetpea Baby Food and Organic Snacks).

Marketing: This is the part of the plan where you let the reader know just how it is you're going to get people to buy your product. We've had many women approach us with business ideas over the years. What we've found is that the marketing plan is one of the most poorly conceived parts of their ideas. When we ask the would-be mompreneurs how they are going to market their businesses, we often hear the answer, "word of mouth." Most likely you'll need to promote your company beyond your word-of-mouth efforts. You need a solid, practical plan for marketing your product or service. (We'll have more to say on the benefits and limitations of a word-of-mouth strategy as you read on.)

WHY EVERYONE NEEDS A MARKETING PLAN

You will need to invest in marketing if you want to grow your business beyond your immediate circle. Word of mouth is terrific, but you can't rely on it for your whole marketing initiative. You need a plan because you need to integrate the different aspects of how your customers relate to your product—its features, its price, how and where they buy it, and how you communicate its benefits and encourage people to try it. If these things aren't in synch—for example, if your product is expensive but sold through discount retail outlets, or your product is complicated to understand but you want to sell it online—then you're likely to be disappointed in the attention that customers pay to your product.

—Prof. Reuber

We spoke to some mompreneurs who started their businesses without a marketing plan. Samantha Rosenberg of Kitsel, an on-line store for baby and toddler clothing, laughs as she recalls, "The only thing I worried about when I started was what I was going to do with all the extra money. I thought I'd build the site, the people would come, and I'd make lots of money." Within a few months, Samantha re-evaluated her thinking and came up with a plan to market Kitsel, and today she runs a very successful online business.

THE FOUR Ps OF MARKETING

In business school, we learned the marketing basics—that is, the mix of things a company can think about to get a customer to buy its product or service. A Harvard Business School professor conveniently boiled down the theory to the four Ps, and it's these elements that you need to think about to develop your marketing plan:

Product—what you sell
Pricing—how much you sell it for
Placement—where you sell it
Promotion—how you get the word out

Another mompreneur told us about her failed experience: "I had no idea about the business or plan. I never thought about how we'd make money or attract customers. With no business background I just thought I'd build my site and the people would come. I did no research about marketing my business."

Maybe you're going to distribute flyers in your neighbourhood. Maybe you have a large-scale advertising plan in place. In our case, our plan had three prongs. We would: (1) attend craft shows to get the product in front of the eyes of customers, (2) engage in PR to tell our story and make our brand visible, and (3) get our product into select retail stores to gain exposure. We included a twelve-month marketing plan in our business plan. It outlined the craft shows we wanted to attend as well as our major PR initiatives. It also outlined the costs associated with each of our ideas. You want to show that you've thought about how to market your business beyond word of mouth.

Operations

This section looks at how you're going to come up with the product you'll be selling. In our case, we needed to look at our fabric suppliers as well as subcontractors and labour for producing our blankets. If you're a service provider, you may want to discuss what goes into providing your service, how long it takes, what the key costs are, etc. In short, you want to show that you have thought about who will produce your product and what it will cost to do so.

Management

Here is your opportunity to show why you're the woman for the job. Discuss your key experiences, strengths, and contacts. You know why you're uniquely positioned to run this business—now let everyone else know too. It's a good idea to include your CV in this section. It shows that you're a serious person with solid work experience. Even if it's a whole new industry for you, it's good to show future investors that you have plenty of experience and that you didn't just fall off the turnip truck.

If you've got partners or other investors, be clear about who owns what and how you've structured the company accordingly.

Funds required and planned use of funds

If you're looking for funding, here is the place to let the reader know how much you're after and what you plan to do with it. Our advice would be to ask right away for more than you think you need. (We can pretty much guarantee you that your costs will be more than you think.) But do lay out clearly how you plan to spend the money. If you're looking for start-up funding, you might list things like office equipment, inventory, marketing, etc. Be specific and connect each cost with an approximate amount. (Double-check your math to make sure it all adds up.)

WHERE TO GO FOR FINANCING

It's a reality that you will have to use some of your own money to start your business. By far, the majority of people use their personal savings, or borrow money from a bank through personal loans, lines of credit, or credit cards. To get a bank loan, you need to have assets (personal or business) that you can use as collateral for the loan. The next most common source of funding is family and friends. These are the people who will give, or lend, you money to start your business because they love you, and not necessarily because they think it will be a huge success. It is possible to get outside investors to invest in your company if it has enormous growth potential, but this happens rarely: fewer than five percent of new businesses are financed by outside investors. Depending on where you live, you might be able to access a government program that provides financial support for new businesses. Websites maintained by different levels of government (national, provincial or state, municipal) can tell you what programs exist. Often these programs are targeted to encourage particular types of entrepreneurs (e.g., youth, Aboriginal) or firms (e.g., technology-based) or to encourage business start-up in economically distressed regions.

—Prof. Reuber

Financial data

....

This is where you dust off your spreadsheet skills and come up with a financial forecast. Not only will you use your financial forecast for your business plan, you'll use it for years to come and you'll never be sorry you did it. Even if you've never done financial forecasting before, it's very doable. (You can also visit our website *www.mominc.ca* to download some forecasting templates.) Whether or not you're going to submit this plan to anyone, this is one of the most important exercises you can do, trust us. This will make you take a good, hard look at your financial reality. Even if the numbers are not pretty—especially if they're not pretty—it's worth it.

There are three key financial statements to prepare: income statement, cash flow statement, and balance sheet.

Income statement

The income statement shows you whether the company is making a profit or losing money. The (extremely) basic formula is this:

$$\text{Revenue} - \text{Expenses} = \text{Profit (or Loss)}$$

Obviously, if you're just starting out you'll need to project these numbers. Be sure to consider all the ways you'll earn revenue as well as the many expenses you'll have. In the financial world, costs are broken into two main categories: Cost of Goods Sold (COGS), which includes the materials and labour that go into making your product; and Selling, General, and Administrative (SG&A), which includes overhead, marketing costs, salaries, etc. Try to think about all of the possible hidden costs that you may not have to worry about yet but that are coming—professional association fees, couriers, credit card fees, bank charges, consultants, technology upgrades, etc. You need as accurate an estimation of your costs as possible.

Many businesses, our own included, overestimate their revenues and grossly underestimate their costs in the early years. Remember how we said we were off the mark on our early numbers? While we did overestimate how quickly our sales would ramp up and even our sales mix (how much of each kind of product we'd sell), where we really missed the mark was on the costs. We failed to consider lots of smaller costs that really add up, and we didn't consider the fact that the more blankets we made, the more we'd have to spend on systems and subcontractors. We'll talk more about the fact that growth costs money, but while you're projecting your costs we'd like to raise the issue.

You'll also need to have a sense of what taxes you'll have to pay, as well as depreciation (the rate at which your assets lose value over time). You can ask your accountant to help you with these. If you don't have an accountant, put this book down and get one.

TIP: GET IN THE BANKER'S SHOES
It is widely said that banks tend to halve the revenues and double the costs when evaluating your financial projections—so you may want to keep this in mind when preparing your business plan.

Cash flow statement

The cash flow statement is a summary of cash receipts and disbursements over a period of time. The (extremely) basic formula is this:

$$\text{Cash collected} - \text{Cash paid out} = \text{Cash available}$$

Looking at cash flow helps you answer the question "Do I have enough cash to continue to operate this business?" Most business owners would agree that cash flow is the most important issue for survival.

STRONG CASH FLOW CAN MAKE OR BREAK YOU

Cash is the fuel needed to run your business. When you run out of gas, your car won't go anywhere. When you run out of cash, your business won't go anywhere. You need cash to pay for material, employees, advertising, even your telephone and Internet bills. When you have lots of cash coming into your company, you have the financial resources to take advantage of opportunities that come your way. For example, you'll have the money to pay for the extra material and labour needed for an unexpected big order. Other people (including your banker) will see your business as a success and will be willing to help you out. If you're short on cash and having trouble paying your bills, though, it will be harder for you to take advantage of opportunities. Unpaid suppliers and employees may not want to extend extra credit to you. People may start to have doubts about your company, and question your decisions or the attractiveness of your market.

—Prof. Reuber

While we're discussing it, managing cash is a huge part of getting your business off the ground. Just because you have assets in your business doesn't mean you can pay your bills. For example, our sales are more heavily weighted in the winter season—which means that we are spending heavily to build up inventory during the summer, our quietest season. We need to make sure that we have the cash available to build our inventory and pay our overhead when our sales are at their lowest.

If you're in the service industry, maybe you have a long lead time before you're paid by your clients. You need to be able to keep afloat while you wait for the paycheque. We know of mompreneur companies that are doing great in terms of sales but are teetering on the edge of disaster because of cash flow problems. Running your own cash flow analysis is a great exercise to help avoid the pitfalls in your particular business model. You can visit our website at www.mominc.ca to download a template for a cash flow statement.

Balance sheet

Even if you don't have a business background, you've probably heard of this one. A balance sheet is a snapshot of the worth of your company at a particular point in time. Unlike the other financial statements, you will create your balance sheet to reflect a certain day rather than the activity of a whole year. So, you won't be forecasting ahead, but rather preparing your balance sheet to reflect your business on the day you create it. The (extremely) basic formula is this:

$$Assets - Liabilities = Equity$$

Your assets are quite simply the things you own or that are owed to you and that you can reasonably expect to collect. Assets are typically broken down into current assets—things you can liquidate quickly (cash in the bank, inventory, accounts receivable, etc.)

and fixed assets—things you can't liquidate quickly (land, computers, etc.). Liabilities are broken down into current liabilities—things that you'll be paying for within the year (accounts payable, short-term loans, taxes payable) and long-term liabilities (long-term loans, mortgage). The balance sheet shows the reader what value your business currently has in it, and anyone who lends you money is going to want to know what you've got to back it.

Appendices

You're almost done—just the appendices to go. Basically, you want to keep your business plan brief and easy to get through. Remember we talked about our marketing plan? Well, we referenced it in the marketing section, but we actually included it in the appendices. Same goes for our CVs. We also included our catalogue. (It was hand-drawn—not the slickest thing you've ever seen, but it was the best we had at the time.)

Other things that you could include in your appendices are press clippings, letters of reference, personal financial data, any legal contracts pertinent to your business (leases, employee contracts, etc.), and organizational charts. Basically, if it will help the reader get a clearer sense of the fact that your company is a good bet, then it doesn't hurt to include it.

LOOKS CAN KILL

You don't have to blow your brains out on the presentation of your business plan. But if you're planning to show it to anyone outside your immediate family, do spend the time to make sure it's checked for spelling and consistent formatting. There are even free templates easily found online to help you make it look great. Your business plan is one of the first impressions people will get of your business and your level of commitment to it.

So those are the basics of a business plan. Now go and do yours! Yes, this exercise will take you some time, but not that much time. And we promise, you'll get out of it what you put in.

There are tons of resources online to help you through the business-plan process, along with some terrific books on the subject if you've got the time and inclination to read them. Even if you don't want to invest the time to do a whole formal plan, why not jot down the key points under each of the "text" sections? But do the financials—it'll be worth your while. If you don't know how, then get some help. No matter what line of work you're getting into and no matter what your background, you're going to need to be in touch with the financial aspect of your business.

9

Getting down and dirty with the digits

Shedding light on some financial concepts

There are some things they teach you in business school that you might not come across otherwise, so we'd like to take a moment to chat about a few important financial concepts. If you're a business-minded gal, bear with us. And if you're not, then hopefully we can share a few thoughts that will save you some anguish down the road.

Cash cycle

Cash cycle, also called the cash conversion cycle, refers to the length of time between purchasing your raw materials and receiving cash from the sale of the finished product. Depending on what your business does and how you do it, managing your cash cycle could become a major issue in your business. Essentially, you may be shelling out for your good or service for months before you actually receive any cash. This has been known to sink companies, so you'll need to make sure that your cash cycle is short enough that you can cover your costs before you get paid. You'll notice that some suppliers want payment on delivery, and nearly every supplier will penalize for payment after thirty days (the length of your terms depends on what you agree to when you set up the relationship). This is because they're making sure that they can meet their cash obligations. It makes sense, doesn't it?

Break-even analysis

Breaking even means that your sales are equal to the costs required to deliver your product. But just to be clear, having your revenue match your expenses on a particular project is not necessarily the same as breaking even. We've been to countless consumer shows where we've met vendors who figure that if their sales matched the cost of exhibiting at the show then they'd broken even. Not so. For example, if the show costs $2,000 and they sell $2,000 worth of merchandise, they have not broken even. Worse, they have actually lost money.

How come? You have to take into account your profit margin and the fact that it costs you something to deliver your product. If you're selling a trinket for $20 that costs you $10 to make, then you need to sell two to "make" $20. We know that you *know* this, but we want to remind you to keep it firmly in mind.

Sales:	$2,000
Less cost of show:	$2,000
Less manufacturing costs:	$1,000
Net profit/loss:	–$1,000

While we're on the subject of breaking even, have you thought about doing some break-even analysis? What we're talking about is creating a spreadsheet (you can get one online if you aren't comfortable making your own) where you can adjust the numbers to see what it's going to take to break even. Basically, you're looking to find the point where your costs equal your sales. From there, you can figure out what happens if things go better or worse than planned by changing your assumptions about sales and costs. It's a great idea to know what you have to do to *not* be losing money. Otherwise, you just might find yourself financing a very expensive hobby.

Being profitable versus making a living

We want to raise the point that being profitable is not the same as making a living. One of the things we commonly heard from mompreneurs is that they're not exactly getting rich off their businesses. But they also told us that their businesses are making money. So what gives?

Three things: The first is that you're profitable if your total sales are $100 and your total costs are $99.99. Profitable—yes; rich—no. The second is the difference between net income and cash flow: just because your income statement says you're profitable doesn't mean that you're necessarily cash positive. Finally, even if your business makes a healthy profit, there is the matter of reinvesting for growth. Growth costs money. Whether you want to undertake new marketing initiatives, invest in better systems, or develop new products, it can be costly to take your business to the next level, and the next one, and the one after that. And when you're just starting out, how do you pay for all that growth? Read on.

Reinvesting for growth and what to pay yourself

Ahem . . . seems we've bumped up against that tricky personal finance stuff again. Well, it's your business so you should get paid what you want, right? You might think so. After all, you've chosen to become a mompreneur to take more control of your life. The reality is that a whole pile of people will need to be paid before you—like your suppliers and employees. If you pay yourself first, and aren't able to pay the others, then you just won't be in business for very long. Either that or you'll be working in the dark from not having paid your electricity bill.

If you do have money left over at the end of the month (or year . . . or five years), then you'll be faced with a decision: do you take out the money for yourself, or reinvest it in your company.

We're not ashamed to tell you that we barely took a penny out of our business in the early years—our business made money from the first year—but we plowed every cent of it into growing our business further. One day we went to hear a talk given by Sandra Wilson, founder of Robeez, and widely considered the "Mother of all Mompreneurs." She told the audience that she didn't withdraw money from her company for the first five years. And she had a heck of a product and brand. (Our relief was palpable.)

Now, many experts will tell you that you should pay yourself right away—and we're not disagreeing with the wisdom of that advice. But be aware that taking out your profits in the way of salary for yourself may mean borrowing money for growth. For us, we equated this with basically paying interest on our own salaries. Since we had worked out our family finances to live without a contribution on our part for a few years, we put everything back into the business early on.

What should you do? It all depends on what works for you, your finances, and your business. You need to spend money to make money, but it's up to you to decide when and how you do that. There is no set amount that a mompreneur should make, so you will just have to do what's best for you, your family, and your business. If you're aiming for a big business, then debt is going to be a part of your life, so you may as well get used to it. Make the choice that works for you on this one. But keep in mind that just because your company is doing well, it doesn't necessarily mean that you're personally laughing all the way to the bank.

Return on investment

While we're having fun with financial concepts, here's another one: return on investment (ROI). In other words, are your activities paying off? There are formulas to work this out, but in simple terms we're suggesting that you take the time to track the results of the things you spend money on. To do this, you have to make sure you have a way to know how your customers get to you. At Admiral Road, we never let a customer leave a phone or web order without finding out how they found us. This information helps us to figure out the return on each of our shows, PR efforts, and other marketing initiatives.

Victoria Sopik is another believer in the importance of tracking results. According to Victoria, her company has "all kinds of metrics in place. We track everything. Who calls, who comes into our daycare centres, who we call. One of the biggest things that most entrepreneurs don't do is to track—but it's how you learn what's successful. We've been astounded at what we've learned."

Joanne Schneeweiss of KidsAroundCanada.com has this to say about how she tracks her results: "My business is online so it's very easy to track what's going on. I check my web traffic statistics everyday. I can see what's working and what's not."

One of the difficulties of tracking your results can be the time lag in customer response. For example, we still see orders from a big PR hit we had five years ago. (God bless the enduring quality of information on the Internet.) You won't know the results of a one-off marketing initiative right away. But we can tell you with a fair bit of accuracy the percentage of our new customers that come from specific initiatives we've done in the past.

The value of a customer

The gestation phase of your business also involves understanding what you're looking for in a customer. This will depend on what kind of business model you have. Whenever we go to a show for Admiral Road or do PR or even just send out a blanket as a gift, we are looking to acquire new customers. But we don't just want customers who are going to order from us once. We are looking for customers who are going to make us their baby gift of choice—who will send a blanket to each of their friends for the next few years when everyone they know is having a baby. Their friends will, in turn, receive our blankets and become our customers too. We know that one-third of our new business comes from people who have received a gift from our company—so the multiplying effect is important. In other words, we're looking for a recurring revenue stream. Not only is it nice to have customers come back time and time again, it also makes the money you've spent to acquire that customer (we're getting to that) a much better investment.

Now, if you're the ShamWow guy (or gal), you'll want to sell as many ShamWows to as many people as you possibly can at a particular trade show. With all due respect to the ShamWow, it's an impulse buy. Either the customer will buy it on the spot or they won't. For that company, it's not a matter of recurring revenue stream. It's a matter of selling ShamWows at as many trade shows as possible. It's all in understanding your business model.

We once did a weekend show and were disappointed by our sales over the three days we were there. Not only were our sales weak, but the customers at the show didn't seem to "get" our product. But then the most amazing thing happened: as soon as we got home, customers from that show started placing orders. Even though it wasn't looking good while we were standing around in a field at the show, that group of customers just needed to go home and think about it.

Once you've completed a marketing initiative, calculate how much business you derived from it and compare it to how much money you spent on it. Even if you think you have an idea of how something went, running the numbers can be surprising and extremely informative.

The cost of a customer

While we're talking about measuring the results of your marketing efforts, it's a good time to think about customer acquisition costs (also sometimes called conversion costs). In our view, this is one of the top things that mompreneurs don't think about when starting up their businesses. If we're being honest, we didn't think much about it either. Now, if you're in the early days of your business, it's hard to know what these costs are, but we do want to point out that there is a cost to acquiring a customer.

Remember what we said about people with plans to grow their business by word of mouth alone? Wouldn't it be nice if that worked? After all, word of mouth is pretty economical! The truth is that you'll need to spend money (on advertising, PR, or other marketing initiatives) to attract new customers. You'll try a few things (and hopefully not too many) that will fail. Others will succeed, but all will cost you money and time. At this point, you probably haven't even thought of half the things you will try to market your business, let alone what will succeed and what will fail. But do yourself a favour and please don't overlook this key cost when thinking about the financial viability of your business.

CALCULATING THE COST OF A CUSTOMER
There's a simple formula to determine the cost to acquire a customer—just divide the total cost of a marketing initiative by the total number of conversions

(a "conversion" can be a lead, a sale, or a purchase). For example, if you spend $750 to run an ad, and as a result find fifty new customers, your cost is $15 to acquire each customer. Of course it's not an exact science—you never know when the customer learned about you originally or if it was the specific marketing initiative that led to the conversion. But you can definitely get a good sense of what your average customer costs you. By thinking about marketing projects this way, you may actually rethink some of your plans. It may turn out that some projects are cheaper for acquiring customers than others.

How much should it cost to acquire a customer? It depends on how much revenue you can derive over the life of the customer. It's all relative.

—Prof. Reuber

Sunk costs

And here's just one more thing we'd like you to keep in mind while we're wading through the murky waters of financial concepts— sunk costs. You've probably heard this term. It basically refers to money you've already spent and can't get back.

Sunk costs have a way of encouraging poor decisions. Think about it—if you've already invested $10,000 in a new venture (product, initiative, market, etc.), it can be pretty hard to walk away. The thinking becomes, "I'll just try this one more thing. After all, I've already spent so much and I don't want to lose it." Your grandma would probably call this line of reasoning "throwing good money after bad." One of the most frustrating things about being an entrepreneur is that you have little idea of how successful your next project is going to be until you try it (i.e., spend money on it). We all make informed guesses on what will work. Sometimes things go the way we hoped, but then sometimes they don't. The key is to not base the decision to spend more money on what you've already spent. Put it behind you, and consider future investments based on future return, not past investments.

Volumes have been written about the fundamentals of business, and if you're keen to learn more we encourage you to read up. In the meantime, we hope we've provided you with a little food for thought.

10

A mompreneur's work is never done

Ongoing business planning

Now that you've got your business plan in hand, we want to point out the important distinction between writing a business plan and engaging in ongoing business planning. A business plan is a document that you draft at a certain point in time. It's static. We recognize that a business plan becomes obsolete the moment you write it—targets move, goals change, realities set in. This is where ongoing planning comes in. The only way you'll keep your business plan *alive* is with ongoing planning.

All the mompreneurs we met think about their businesses and what they want from them often, but not necessarily in any structured way. Single mom of one, Quita Alfred of InQb8 quilts has this to say about her experience: "I had a business plan at the outset, but I didn't do ongoing planning. If I had I think I would have changed courses earlier. Instead, I scrambled and lost interest in my business." In truth, your business plan should go hand-in-hand with ongoing business planning. It's going to be tough to execute one without the other.

Okay, so you've got your plan and you have a Big Picture vision for your company. Now what? Well, it's time to do some shorter-term business planning. And this should be just the beginning of your love affair with forward thinking for your business.

Unlike ol' Dwight, we like the plan and the planning, but if you must choose, then do the latter.

We asked mompreneurs about their experiences with business planning. Nicole Garza of Mally Designs admits that strategy and planning were initially overshadowed by so many other tasks. Now she has a very strategic marketing plan, planned one year in advance, which includes specific dates for various marketing activities such as new design and product launches, events, social media activity, and other marketing plans.

We thought that mompreneur Micheline Courtemanche, mom of three girls and owner of Betty and Bing Letterpress, had a really interesting perspective on her lack of planning. Micheline says, "I wish I did some planning so I would know how much work is 'enough.' If I had a clear sense of how much work I needed then I would feel less stress and guilt. I would know when I needed to look for work and when I could turn it away."

We haven't talked much yet about balancing the business with your family—but knowing how much work you need to take on to meet your financial needs is key when you've got the demands of family competing with the business.

Some mompreneurs have been hardcore planners from Day One. Sarah Morgenstern and Minnow Hamilton of SavvyMom.ca took their planning very seriously. According to Sarah, "We did a lot of planning. We spent days on end in Minnow's kitchen doing everything from our business plan to figuring out childcare plans." That it took exactly nine months of planning and preparation to launch their business is not lost on these two moms!

Ongoing planning: Our story

We get together early in the year for a big planning session. This makes sense for our business, as Christmas is our biggest season and we are starting fresh in January. We have what we call the "G2 Summit." (The "group," of course, is the two of us.) For several days we lock ourselves away from phones and kids and talk about what we want from the business in the upcoming year. We think about our business in terms of several key categories: products and production, marketing, and administration. We start with an agenda of things we each want to discuss, and when we're done we come up with a month-by-month action plan and assign responsibility to each actionable point. We also try to have a weekly check-in with each other to see where we are with our plans.

Don't have a partner? No problem. Have a G1 Summit. Take yourself to your local coffee shop and dedicate yourself to thinking about what you want out of the period coming up. Divide your thinking into the relevant categories and make your own action plan. What we've heard from the women we've talked to is that working alone seems to make planning harder. We can definitely sympathize. If you can't bring yourself to do it alone, then find a sympathetic listener (your husband, best friend, mom, or professional mentor are good candidates) and ask them to work through the plan with you.

Goal setting

Tied up with the idea of planning for your business on a regular basis is goal setting. If the plan is the road map, then the goal is the destination. What do you want from your business? Your family? Your life? Basically, if you don't know where you're going, it's going to be awfully hard to get there.

When we did our MBAs we learned that setting well-thought-out goals is key to success. We were taught this handy (if a little cheesy) acronym: SMART. Dust off your alphabet flash cards—here's the lowdown on SMART goal setting:

S is for Specific

This is the who, what, when, where, and how department. Let's say you want to grow your business. A specific goal would be "I want to grow my business by attracting five new clients from referrals within the next six months" or "I will make five sales calls every day this month."

M is for Measurable

In the business world, and certainly in business school, the following expression is often heard: "That which gets measured gets done." Think about it. We don't know about you, but we're more likely to get something done when there is some external reason for doing it, such as a deadline or a promise to another person. Just telling yourself to do something isn't always enough to motivate you into action. Setting measurable goals can get you moving.

An example of a measurable goal would be "I want to cut ten percent from my costs each month until the end of the year" or "I want to spend two hours of quality time with my son each week."

A is for Attainable

There's no point in setting a goal you can't reach. If you don't have the money or time to meet it, then you'll just be disappointed. Set your goals accordingly.

R is for Realistic

Sure, we wish every baby in the world had an Admiral Road blanket (we truly believe they should). But it's probably more realistic to focus on growing our business in a particular market or in a particular way.

T is for Timely

Give yourself a time frame. Unless you were one of those amazing creatures who did school assignments when they were handed out instead of when they were due, putting a date on the calendar by which to achieve something can be just the kick in the pants you need.

Okay, so they made us learn SMART goals in business school and now we've passed this lesson on to you. Forgive us. What we're really trying to impart is the importance of setting specific goals that you can measure yourself against. Remember: there are no performance evaluations in an entrepreneurial venture—it's up to you to set and meet benchmarks for your whole life—professional and personal.

The mompreneurs we talked to had some creative ways of keeping their goals front of mind. Melissa Arnott, who runs The BabyTime Shows, wrote herself a note when she first started the business outlining what she wanted to accomplish with her business. After each show, Melissa takes the note out and looks at it to see if she is on track with her goals.

Victoria Turner of Pippalily and Simply on Board has a dream board prominently located above her desk—on it are goals varying from sales goals to being on *Oprah*. The mompreneurs at Supper-Works have regular meetings at which they look at where they are compared with their "magic number" and then plan accordingly.

One mompreneur tells us that her goal is for no one in her family but her to realize she has a job. In other words, she wants to be primarily available to her family and doesn't want her work to interfere with that priority ever—so the less her family is aware of her business, the better she's doing at meeting her goals.

It doesn't matter how you keep your goals front of mind—just do it!

It takes a village

Getting help with your business

As you're getting through the gestation period of your business, you might want to consider getting some help thinking about your business. Now, we know you're the foremost expert on your business concept—that's the way it should be! But that doesn't mean you couldn't stand to learn a few things. Today, in our ninth year, we still routinely ask for help when we need it. We bounce ideas off family members or friends, we source suppliers through fellow mompreneurs, and we generally make sure we're on track by checking in with some smart people.

So how do you go about getting some help? In general, we've found the old adage to be true: Ask and you shall receive. There are a number of ways you can think about souping up the brain power working behind your business.

Mentors

There's a lot we stand to learn when we're starting out in business for ourselves. The good news is that many business people have gone before us. You just need to find a way to tap into their expertise.

At Admiral Road, we have always been open to idea-sharing with other mompreneurs, but we have also actively sought the advice of mompreneurs who are ahead of us on the learning curve. In the burgeoning world of mompreneurs, this isn't always easy to find. Some of the mompreneurs we spoke to told us that they were actively seeking a mentor and acknowledged that it can be tough to find someone who is doing the same thing but who is a few years ahead.

May you be blessed with many generous mentors. We mean that. Mentors can save you time and money by teaching you valuable lessons and can generally make you feel less alone in the business world. A mentor can be anyone whose opinion you trust, but your best bet is someone who is in a similar sector but ahead of you on the curve. (This is not dissimilar to finding a close friend or relative who has had a baby a year before you. The advice and the hand-me-downs are invaluable.) The perfect mentor is a mom, of course, who is not threatened by your potential as a business competitor and who is endlessly available to you! If you can find such a mentor—and we know some mompreneurs who have—then count yourself lucky and be sure to pay it forward.

Even if you can't find an exact role model, draw on the different strengths of the people you know. For example, we look to two male entrepreneurs we know for their expertise because they're in a long-standing partnership. We also look to friends at another company for their expertise in marketing innovation. That is, even among the people you know you can find examples of best practices and opportunities to learn.

We certainly wouldn't be where we are today without Pat Scriver. Pat is an old friend of Amy's family's. She founded Courage My Love, the original vintage clothing store in Toronto's Kensington Market, in 1975. A connoisseur of fashion and born bargain hunter, no one knows retail like Pat. In the early days of Admiral Road, we dropped in on Pat for a cup of tea. We showed her our new blanket designs and she provided blunt and honest feedback—the kind of feedback that guided our decision-making about blanket production for years to come. But she also provided more. Pat shared the names of some local home sewers—other mompreneurs who work in the garment industry, and women with whom we still work today. We simply wouldn't have found these women if Pat hadn't made the introductions. And the thing is, she was more than happy to share the information.

In fact, we think you should talk to anyone who knows anything about business. It can't hurt. Even if you don't know anyone in your immediate circle who can help you plan for your mompreneur venture, ask around. People are usually flattered to be considered experienced and wise.

We've never met anyone as good at finding advice as Eryn Green and Tamar Wagman of Sweetpea Baby Food and Organic Snacks. In fact, we got to know them when they called us up and asked if we'd have a coffee with them. In the gestation of their business they spoke to anyone who would talk to them—web people, graphic designers, experienced business folks, and people in the food and baby product industries. They offered up the following advice: "Meet with anyone who will talk to you. You don't have to take their advice, but you should definitely listen to it."

IS ENTREPRENEURSHIP IN YOUR DNA?

Our research suggests that there is something hereditary about entrepreneurship—scores of the mompreneurs we talked to had grown up with at least one entrepreneurial parent. When we delved a little deeper, we found that statistics backed up our theory. According to a 2009 report by the Ewing Marion Kauffman Foundation, nearly half of business founders had a parent who started a small business first. So when it comes to getting guidance, your mom or dad just might have learned a few lessons that they can share with you.

When our business was nothing but a bun in the oven, we had coffee with everyone we knew who had a functioning partnership and asked for advice about our own new partnership. We've also turned to a friend with an established business in a different field for advice about shipping, sourcing, and strategy. And every year or two we find ourselves back on campus in Becky's office to have a strategy session. Feeling sheepish about being a bother? As one of our male entrepreneur friends says, "Just about anyone will take your call. Call them. You're probably a pleasant distraction from their overdue accounts receivable sheet!"

Mentorship doesn't have to be a formal arrangement, although it certainly can be. You can turn to different people for various issues throughout the life of your business. But now is a great time to ask a lot of questions—never will you know less about what you're doing than before you've even opened the door.

Some mompreneurs have even found mentors and friends among what could be considered competitors. Jennifer Torres, the force behind Salsa Babies, called up an established company in a similar sector to ask for some advice in the early days of her business. Here's what she said about the experience: "Andrea Page of Fit-Mom taught me a great lesson. She had an open attitude towards giving me advice from the start. She could have looked at me as a competitor and not helped me. But she has been open and giving." Jennifer has opted to pass on the good karma. She says, "I've really tried to continue that [spirit of helping others]. I've had former students who have launched their own ideas who come to me and I'm happy to help them." Today, Andrea and Jennifer are both colleagues and good friends.

We also loved another of Jennifer's mentorship experiences. She contacted the owner of a long-established dance school in the city where she lives. The owner shared valuable information like how to format registration forms, scheduling, and more, but more importantly she shared that fifteen years earlier she had started her business by putting up flyers while pushing her baby around in the stroller—just like Jennifer. "Seeing how far she has come has really inspired me and made me believe that I can do it too," recalls Jennifer of the experience.

Business coach or consultant

A number of mompreneurs make use of business consultants or coaches. These are experienced business people who have made a career out of listening to entrepreneurs, assisting them in articulating their goals, identifying their obstacles, and helping them map out and achieve success. It's kind of a cross between a sports coach and a therapist for your business.

A business coach should be able to help with everything from developing marketing materials to high-level strategy. She will listen attentively, and most importantly, she will tell you the truth. Your business and your ego are about to be much more closely tied than you can imagine. Your business can feel like an extension of you, so looking at what's not working can be pretty tough. A good coach will tell you the real deal even if it's not what you want to hear. And that is priceless. She will also help you set goals and be someone to whom you will feel accountable. One of the mompreneurs we spoke to suggested that a business coach is invaluable as a sounding board: "You need a confidant and mentor. It's too much to expect of your husband. I hired a business advisor, who I meet with regularly."

It makes you wonder why everyone doesn't have a business coach, right? Well, a major drawback is the price tag. It's not cheap: a one-on-one session can run you $100 to $200 per hour or more, though some coaches charge small businesses less. When finances are tight, paying for someone to listen and talk to you can seem like a luxury you can do without—but if it helps you achieve real results quickly, it may be worth it.

Traci Bisson of The Mom Entrepreneur, a company that provides support and training to mompreneurs, doesn't regret her decision to hire a coach. She says, "My business consultant taught me
so much. If I'd understood these things earlier I may not have made
many of the mistakes I made. I couldn't have learned these things
on my own—I wouldn't have known where to look. It's ironic that
you need to grow your business to a certain size to afford a business coach."

Besides the obvious issue of money, it can also be hard to find
the right fit. Despite Traci's appreciation for her business coach she
concedes, "She's not the ultimate mentor for me because she's not
a mother."

If you're thinking about hiring a business coach, ask lots of questions and make sure she's the right gal for the job. We come across
lots of websites for business coaches that don't actually list any real
business experience. You want to make sure that your coach has
a context for what she's telling you—and that she has a real sense
of the business world. Try to speak to some of her former clients
as well.

How can you find a business coach? It's easy to find websites
where coaches are listed, but your best bet is to ask around and see
if you can get a referral from a friend or colleague.

Advisory boards

A lot of experts suggest that entrepreneurs set up an advisory board to help them with their businesses. An advisory board consists of people who aren't involved with the day-to-day operations of your business. They can provide advice and introductions and be a sounding board for new ideas you're considering. Admittedly, we only know of a handful of mompreneurs who have gone the advisory board route, but if you're looking to raise money to start your business this can be an effective way to get the ball rolling.

So who should be on this board? Advisory boards of start-ups typically consist of between two and four smart people willing to spend some time every few months thinking about your business. Think about gaps in your expertise and the type of knowledge that you need most. Given your druthers, you'd pick people from varying backgrounds who can each bring something different to the table. Know a lawyer? Someone in finance? A successful entrepreneur? Look for people who have what you're lacking. But at the same time, be choosy. Avoid difficult personalities. You want to make sure that the members of your advisory board are people you'd want to sit in a room with. You also want to make sure that each plays well enough with others to be able to sit through a few meetings together and hear each other out. Finally, consider how well-known and influential a potential board member is. Not only are they likely to know a lot, but people will know them and be impressed that someone of that calibre has gotten involved with your business. This can help when you're raising money or trying to convince an organization to take a chance on a start-up firm. In fact, once you have one prestigious board member, it will become easier to recruit others.

But you're not looking for your best friend in this scenario. In fact, the last thing you want is a room full of cheerleaders. You want challenge and inspiration from your advisory board, not a pat on the head.

Elizabeth Kaiden is a freelance journalist. A mom of three, Elizabeth wanted some part-time childcare outside the home in New York City where she lives—which was nearly impossible to come by. She loved the idea of a place where people like her could go with their children, have their children taken care of, and get some work done. She founded Two Rooms as a not-for-profit organization. Here's what happened to Elizabeth when she established a board: "These were four people I knew well. I was comfortable with them. They encouraged me to 'please do it!' My board was the team of people to support my business but not the right people to help get it off the ground."

We all know people are busy, so make sure you're clear about what you're looking for. When you meet in person, have an agenda and stick to it. Also, be sure to distribute important information beforehand. Between in-person meetings, you can have telephone meetings with specific individuals if they're willing to help you out with particular issues during a specified time period. People are more willing to do you a favour and spend more time than expected if they understand the objectives and can see the end in sight.

It's a good idea to have a set term on your advisory board— for example, a term of two years. Potential board members like knowing the extent of their commitment, and it allows you to take someone off gracefully if they're not working out. If it's working for everyone, you can always ask them to stay.

GOING UP?

Ever hear the expression "elevator pitch"? It refers to describing what the unique selling points of your business are—in the length of time it would take you and the listener to reach your floor by elevator. Our elevator pitch would go something like, "Admiral Road makes beautiful, practical personalized baby blankets. Kids love how bright, soft, and cozy our blankets are, while moms love how easy they are to care for. Our customers love how easy it is to order a special keepsake gift."

If you're approaching a potential advisor who isn't familiar with you, give your best elevator pitch, send over your business plan, and don't hesitate to name-drop if you're able to. If you have any connection to someone they know and respect, it's certainly worth mentioning.

Knowing connected and smart people was never bad for anyone's business. Ultimately, smart business people are turned on by great business ideas and inspiring entrepreneurs—if you're prepared and enthusiastic it'll go a long way towards convincing them to take you on.

COMPENSATING YOUR ADVISORY BOARD

In general, an advisory board doesn't receive compensation, but it depends on their time commitment and what they're doing for you. At a minimum, paying for a nice lunch and supplying them with your firm's products or services certainly doesn't hurt. Advisors might agree to come on board in exchange for some equity in the company, and this can provide financial incentives to help your business succeed. If you are starting a larger-scale company and are looking for a committed and experienced advisory board to help the business grow, then these incentives will match yours. However, advisors rarely become involved with new firms because of financial reasons. They may be paying it forward: returning a favour that was once done for them. They may be running a now-established firm and miss the fun and dynamism of starting a company. They may find your business concept intellectually interesting. If they agree to participate, however, you know that they're excited about working with you and the potential of your ideas.

—Prof. Reuber

Whether or not you formalize how you get help with your business, it's smart to surround yourself with smart people. What's true about raising your child holds true for your business too: it takes a village.

12

Your other full-time job

Managing life on the home front

Whatever is going on in your business, you're still the CEO of your family. We've been talking a lot about planning for your business, but are you meeting your life goals as well? If one of the reasons you decided to be a mompreneur was to have more balance and time with your family, then don't forget to make that a measurable, realistic goal. We recommend planning for your life regularly as well as for your business. Whenever you sit down to think about your business, take a look at what you want from the rest of your life. Here are a few of the Biggies you'll need to plan for.

Childcare

Many of the mompreneurs we spoke to told us how important a childcare plan is to the success of their business. And this is one of the paradoxes of the mompreneur experience. You start your company so that you can be available to your children, but as your business grows you'll probably need some childcare so that you can work at it. So what are your choices in this department?

Full-time

Some mompreneurs line up their childcare from the start. This can make a lot of sense. A new business can suck up astounding amounts of time, and having full days to work can be a godsend. On the downside, childcare is usually expensive and it can be hard to budget for childcare when the money is coming in slowly. And if you're not with the little ones, you may find yourself wondering why you didn't just go back to your regular paycheque.

Part-time

Many of the mompreneurs we were in touch with have lined up some part-time care for their kids. Some work half-days or just a few days a week. Sundi Hoffman of Bugalug does the latter: "I couldn't be a full-time mom. I work three days a week from 9:30 a.m. to 3:30 p.m., plus a little here and there. Monday and Friday are family days, and I try not to turn on the computer on the days I spend with my kids. I probably work forty hours a week, but I've only got three designated work days."

For lots of us mompreneurs, this is a great solution—you get to wear your mom hat and your entrepreneur hat every week. Of course this can mean that you're working well into the nights. (We've rarely met a mompreneur who doesn't hit her desk after the kids are in bed.) And again, if you're only working part-time hours (and forty hours is definitely part-time for an entrepreneurial venture), then it's fair to assume you'll earn part-time money.

I think it's fruitless to try to work while the kids are around. It's better to stay up late and get the work done.

—Anita MacCallum, bookkeeper

No childcare

Some think it's ludicrous to try to run a business while your baby is napping—in other words, you can't run a business if your kids are home. Martha Scully of Canadian Sitter, an online Canadian site that helps families find caregivers, puts it this way. "Moms should not be cooking, watching the kids, and doing laundry while starting a business. I think it's the reason some businesses fail. You need to focus."

Here's what we think. You *can* start and run your business while your baby is napping—we did. (Challenging when one of Amy's kids would nap for precisely, but only, fifty-nine minutes each afternoon.) But you need to be prepared to grow your business much more slowly than if you were working at it full-time. We each took tiny maternity leaves and then had the babies with us full-time until well into their second year. This meant propping up their bouncy chairs on the studio work table, schlepping them around to suppliers, and popping in the Baby Einstein video when need be. It also meant that business stopped when the babies were hungry or needed to be changed or otherwise attended to. It meant we worked less at our mutual office space and more at our respective homes. Overall, it meant we were less efficient at our business and probably not so efficient at motherhood either—but it gave us the chance to have one foot in each life and it worked for us. We both started our oldest children in part-time daycare in their second year, and followed suit with the kids who came later.

Keep in mind that your child's needs are going to change, as are your own. That little baby who naps twice a day (God willing) will eventually stop napping. And she won't always be content to bounce in her chair next to you while you work the hours away. Whatever you work out for childcare, we can't stress enough the need to constantly assess how it's working for everyone and to be flexible enough to make changes.

However you're going to set up your childcare arrangement, we can pretty much promise you that each and every week you'll find yourself trying to get work done while the kids are around. So what's a mompreneur to do? We asked around, and here's what we came up with.

Keeping a healthy perspective

Being a mompreneur means being flexible if nothing else. At Admiral Road, we think about what we need to get done in a given week, or month. Our goal was always to work part-time. That means some days are Mommy Days and no work gets done at all. And sometimes a kid gets sick or your childcare arrangement blows up in your face and your workday just doesn't go as planned. That's why we like to think about what work needs to get done on a more "macro" level. If we thought about the business tasks we needed to do day by day, we would just get frustrated. But if you think about what needs to get done in broad strokes, it will be easier to squeeze in the work after the kids have gone to bed—or whenever else you can find the time.

CALCULATE THE TIME YOU HAVE AVAILABLE FOR WORK
Do the math on the actual number of hours you have to dedicate to your business each week. Look at your week and deduct the time you spend with your family, getting kids to school, preparing meals, doing laundry, vol-

unteering in the classroom, going to the gym, and sleeping, and see what you've got left over for work. It may not be much! But on the flip side, you may be encouraged by how much you have accomplished in just a handful of hours per week. Knowing how much time you need and want to spend with your kids, be realistic about how much time you can dedicate to your business each week. You might be a little kinder to yourself if you are reasonable about your expectations.

—Debbi Arnold, DA Consulting

Scheduling work time

When it comes to scheduling time for work, the mompreneurs we spoke to were very inventive. Some paid for full-time daycare only to use it part-time. This allowed them backup for contingencies, but still let them spend time with their kids during the day on a regular basis. One smart mom told us that she has her sitter start at 2 p.m. one day a week. That arrangement allows her to spend the morning with the kids and even permits a date night with her husband.

Working after the kids go to bed seems to be a coping mechanism for nearly every mompreneur we spoke to. It's just part of the deal.

Another tip of the trade is to really focus on the task at hand. Diane Flacks, a mother of two boys, writer, and actor told us, "I'm surprised at my ability to focus in a small amount of time. It's amazing what you can get done in twenty minutes. Your time is valuable and you know it."

TIP: DESIGNATE ONE DAY A WEEK AS "MEETING DAY"
I spend the time to get dressed properly and let my family know what to expect. I meet with everyone I need to on that one day, and the rest of the week is for ponytails and wearing lululemon.

—Melissa Arnott, The BabyTime Shows

And finally, it's easy to become so immersed in your business that you lose sight of the reason you wanted flexibility in the first place: to spend more time with your kids. The mompreneurs we met told us that they make a point of being available to their kids whenever they can. One mom told us, "I make myself take time off when my kids are off school for holidays or PA days. I remind myself, 'This is why I do this.'"

Finding "Me Time"

Many mompreneurs will actually laugh if you bring up the notion of Me Time. After all, you're juggling a business and a family. Regrettably, you also need to sleep, eat, and bathe. But here's the thing—if you don't plan for (and insist on) at least a little time for yourself, there may be some pretty serious repercussions. You know what they say about all work and no play, right? We think that caring only for your business and your kids can make you downright batty—and what's worse, it can make you lose interest in your business. If your business becomes the thing that keeps you from your other interests you just may learn to resent it.

Alison Lim of Style Kid, an online children's retailer, shares her perspective: "You have to be a wife, mother, entrepreneur, chauffeur, housekeeper, cook—it's a constant juggle. We put ourselves last. You can become depressed and wonder whether it's worth it. I didn't have any time for myself for a long time—but I found that I didn't have any patience. Now I take time out—the kids may get less of my time, but I'm a better mom and wife because of it. I do all the business travel by myself. I learned that I love being on my own. I even add a day onto the end of a business trip for myself—it's great."

Melissa Arnott was the subject of a Me Time intervention. She says, "I was working all the time. Then, an old friend of mine knocked on my door one night and insisted that I go out with her for a glass of wine. (She had already spoken to my husband.) She said she loved what I was doing but that I needed not to lose myself in it. I was lucky she did that."

Many mompreneurs tell us that the business is their Me Time. We told ourselves that for a long time too. After all, compared with rocking a colicky baby or wading through a diaper disaster, sitting down at your desk can feel like a day at the spa! But we have learned over time that taking time to do whatever it is that makes you feel sane is important. Sure, your business is going to lose out on you in those few hours you steal for yourself, but think how much longer you're going to be energized for both your business and your family if you can take a bit of time to nurture yourself.

The mompreneurs we talked to had a few different strategies for inserting some sanity time in their lives. Many were keen on scheduling it in. Author, television personality, and public speaker (plus busy mom of four) Kathy Buckworth tells us, "I schedule everything— gym time, a pedicure, whatever. I do find Me Time, but I find it hard not to feel guilty about it. You need the time out of the office—but releasing the guilt is hard."

TIP: TRICKS FOR KEEPING THE BALLS IN THE AIR
Disclaimer: Don't think for a second we do all of these things all of the time—but we do find that life is easier when we follow these tips.

Danielle: A monthly meal plan. I've been known to fall off the wagon, but having a monthly meal plan saves me time and money at the grocery store, removes the stress of thinking about what's for dinner, and avoids the 4 p.m. *everything-is-frozen* panic.

Amy: Date night at home. No matter what else is going on in the week, I always have dinner with my husband on Friday nights after the kids have gone to bed. Not only can we catch up on any child- or house-related issues, we also get a chance to connect with each other.

Danielle: Buy greeting cards in bulk. I try to make a list of every birthday card I'll need within a year and buy them all at once. That way I'm never scrambling to get to a store at the last minute.

Amy: A present box. I have a space at home where I stash away several months' worth of toys for birthday presents. With three girls, there is no shortage of birthday parties, so I try to make sure I've got gifts for the ages of each child's friends.

Danielle: Personal calls in the car. I'm in the car for work quite a bit, so I use that time to make (hands-free) phone calls to friends and family. I don't have much time during the workday, but my car time allows me to stay in touch.

Amy: Schedule everything in Outlook. I schedule all work and personal appointments in Microsoft Outlook. I can share upcoming appointments with Danielle or my husband and I receive on-screen reminders when events are upcoming.

Victoria Sopik of Kids & Company applies her fifty-percent rule to time for herself. She says, "There are people I know who accomplish half as much as I do in terms of enjoying life. They need for everything to be perfect. I know lots of women who haven't entertained in years because they can't do it perfectly. I'm fine with paper plates! I decide what I can and want to commit to something and then I'm good with that. I'm happy to do things at fifty percent."

The wisest of mompreneurs also manage to schedule date nights to stay connected with their partners. We'll get into the relationship between your business and your mate a bit later, but suffice it to say that it's important to plan for all aspects of your life, and your life partner is certainly a big one.

Setting up workspace

Getting organized in terms of physical space is key to managing the combination of work and motherhood. Traci Bisson, of The Mom Entrepreneur told us: "Setup is important. My desk is next to the playroom. Being able to be in the same room has helped. They know not to disturb me when I'm on a call. I've also moved most of my business online—it's much easier to work online than by phone or in-person when balancing motherhood. I think it was easier when my kids were babies—you can schedule around their sleep schedule. Also, my kids were in daycare during the toddler years when kids really need a lot of time and attention. I think you have to choose the business you want based on your kids."

In fact, many of the mompreneurs we spoke to told us that they had set up their work stations so they could be physically close to the kids, with many reporting that adding a computer in the kitchen has helped stay in touch with business while being with the family.

Amusing the kids when you have to work

Of course setting up to be near the kids doesn't mean that the kids aren't going to want a piece of you! In our experience, it can be pretty hard for the kids to understand that you aren't available to them when they can see you, even if you're sitting at your desk.

Lots of mompreneurs get their kids in on the action. By giving Junior a "job" in the business, or at least the perception of a job, you can usually buy yourself a bit of time. Now who's kidding who? We know that this will likely take more of your time than is merited by the "help," but it does show the kids that you're working and lets them have a sense of belonging in your professional life.

Other moms save their very best toys or crafts for those moments when they really need to keep the kids busy and get some work done. In our experience, if playdough isn't served up regularly, you can buy yourself a good hour by pulling it out!

Many mompreneurs won't take or make phone calls when the kids are home. After all, every mom knows that you're never more desirable or indispensable to your children than the second after you've picked up the phone. That being said, sometimes the call has to be dealt with. Some of the women we spoke to reported locking themselves in the bathroom or hiding in a closet! Truth be told, most of your clients are parents too and are going to understand the occasional background noise.

Multi-tasking—working and parenting at the same time

Nearly every single mompreneur we spoke to told us that she uses technology to allow herself to be in two "places" at once. Smartphones and BlackBerrys may be a mompreneur's best friend. While it's true you can become tied to them, having one really lets you take your business on the road. One mompreneur advises making the investment, even though it can be steep, because it saves you money in the long run. And according to celebrity gifter Julie Kenney of Jewels and Pinstripes, technology can make mompreneurship a walk in the park: "Having a BlackBerry and other technology helps a lot. I've gotten really good at texting while pushing a stroller!"

We thought the tips from mompreneurs were really helpful. In fact, they inspired us to come up with this list:

Ten things a mompreneur can't live without (or that at least are really good to have)

1. A good husband or life partner
2. A business partner
3. A childcare provider
4. A business plan
5. A dedicated phone line
6. A BlackBerry or smartphone
7. A good support system
8. A mentor
9. Some dedicated workspace
10. A sense of humour

For so many of us, balance, availability to our children, and time for things other than work are a huge part of the rationale for starting our own businesses. A new business can suck up an incredible amount of your inner and outer resources, so don't forget to plan for the things you want from your new life.

PART 4

BIRTH AND THE FIRST YEAR:
CONGRATULATIONS—IT'S A BUSINESS!

Nothing can ever compare to the day your child is born—a life-altering moment after which nothing is ever the same again. Your business may not hold for you the same emotional significance, but there are still many parallels between birthing your children and birthing your business. In both cases, you've planned, conceived, and gestated. Both cases involve hard work, pain, and joy. And just like with an actual baby, now the real work in your business begins! In this section, we'll focus on your newborn business and all the things you'll want to give her to set her up for life.

13

Watching your pennies

Budgeting and spending wisely

Maybe you've got a few dollars to spend on your new business, or maybe you've got millions. Regardless of what your start-up budget is, there are ways you can think about how to spend your hard-won dollars wisely.

When your start-up budget is small, it's easy to watch it vanish quickly. When we first set up our business telephone lines, the phone company claimed ten percent of our start-up budget! (Each of our home telephone lines happened to be in our husbands' names. Because neither one of us had an account in our own name at the time, the phone company harshly penalized us, requiring a twelve-month security deposit of $750 in addition to the exorbitant fees to set up our services. Don't even get us started on that injustice.) But even when your budget is larger, there are ways to evaluate where to best spend your dollars. This chapter will address ways to approach your budget.

Overhead and administration spending

When it came time for us to set up shop at Admiral Road, we looked at what was left of our budget after we bought the blanket business and figured out how far we could stretch it. We eliminated the need to pay rent by working out of Amy's dad's basement to start. We needed to spend money to design a logo, buy a computer, and set up phone lines and a website. We needed to buy fabric and sewing machines and have some cash left to pay our sewers. We also needed money to apply to craft shows since that is how we planned to market ourselves. As we mentioned, we didn't initially budget on paying ourselves.

At Admiral Road, we happen to be very . . . er . . . frugal. We started up our business for $15,000. We just couldn't imagine investing any more than that. But that start-up investment was also consistent with the kind of business we wanted to grow: a crafty, home-based cottage industry. We have subcontractors and suppliers all over the city, but to this day, we still work out of our homes. It works for the business and for our families.

DETERMINING YOUR START-UP INVESTMENT

Higher growth aspirations require larger investments in time, people, partnerships, products, and investments. Want to keep things small? Looking to conquer the world? Plan to invest accordingly.

—Prof. Reuber

Like us, mompreneurs Elisa Palter and Shari Wert started with a very modest budget. But unlike us, they wanted to project a large, corporate image, despite the fact that they were working from Elisa's basement. Their idea was to create *Help! We've Got Kids*, a resource directory of products and services for parents. They needed to court their customers, who happened to be booksellers and publishers. They didn't have any trouble achieving the desired image, even on small budget. Elisa says, "We each put in $5,000 to start and we didn't use it up. (We were profitable in our first year.) We knew that we needed to look bigger than we were—that we needed the appearance of real company."

FIVE WAYS TO START A BUSINESS FOR UNDER $1,000

When surfing the blogosphere, we came across the following post and absolutely loved it. Heather Allard, author, business coach, and owner of The Mogul Mom, a website and newsletter for mompreneurs, echoes our beliefs about how and when to spend. She writes:

In 2004, I started a company to bring my inventions, Swaddleaze and Blankeaze, to market.

I spent money like a rock star. Out of the gate, I spent:

$15,000 on a website with a custom shopping cart that didn't work
$2,000 for a logo that looked more like a Kama Sutra position than a
symbol of safe sleepwear for infants
$1,300 on stationery and business cards
$2,000 on a merchant account setup and monthly fees
$1,000 on PR leads
$12,000 on a publicist
$17,000 on advertising in magazines
$4,000 on Google AdWords

_____

$54,300

I spent almost $54,000 and that didn't even include product manufacturing. Who did I think I was? Kimora Lee Simmons? If I started my company now, I'd do things so differently. I could start a business for under $1,000 if I did these five things:

1. **Skip the website:** I'd scrap the website with custom shopping cart by creating a self-hosted blog and hook it up to a PayPal account.

2. **Hire a freelancer:** Instead of hiring a "big company" to create a logo, I'd find a freelancer.

3. **Go DIY:** I'd "Do it yourself" as many things as I could. Here are just a few of the things I could do very easily:
   - Create business letterhead using readily available free online software.
   - Pitch the media on my own.
   - Choose three to five keywords and use free search engine optimization software and SEO the heck out of my site.
   - Set up Google Analytics on my site so I can track who's visiting, what they're reading, who referred them, and more.

4. **Become a social butterfly:** I'd start networking on blogs and social media sites to build interest in my new site and develop the reputation as a knowledgeable, helpful person in my field.

5. **Use Free stuff:** I'd use as many free services as possible until my business warranted paid services. Just some of the ways I'd grow my business without spending a cent: create surveys, track contacts and leads, send sales and marketing emails, edit and manage photos, analyze web traffic, and more—all using free online software.

    —Heather Allard, TheMogulMom.com

For a list of the free online software Heather is referring to, visit our website at www.mominc.ca.

Mabel's Labels was run for years out of Cynthia Esp's home. It made of lot of sense: rent was cheap and she skipped paying for daycare since she was available to care for her young children.

The frugality paid off, and last year Mabel's Labels moved into a 5,000-square-foot warehouse space to have room for inventory and up to thirty staff members. By keeping its start-up capital for the real essentials, Mabel's Labels was able to grow to a size where the business could pay for large-scale expansion.

Trish Magwood, a mom of three, TV personality, and author, owned and operated Dish, a high-end cooking studio, café, and catering company. Having recently sold her business, Trish tells us, "Knowing what I know now, I would advise people to go easy with overhead. It's easy to get caught up in the physical space—but it's also expensive! I think that I spent more money than I ought to have on that aspect."

We've met few mompreneurs more ambitious than Victoria Sopik. Her idea to build a $50 million corporate daycare chain was intensely expensive. Needing physical space in prime locations, her overhead spending is massive. Despite the need to spend aggressively when she was starting out, Victoria was still budget-conscious. She worked from home instead of spending to have a fancy office out of the house. If Victoria could revolutionize the childcare industry from her home office, you can probably curb your overhead spending too.

In terms of spending, overhead is a biggie (and unavoidable if you're opening a brick-and-mortar operation). Do yourself a favour by thinking about the things you need to spend money on versus the things you want to spend money on. For example, we knew that we needed appropriate marketing materials, but we didn't want to blow the bank. We didn't print Admiral Road business cards or stationery for years. Seriously—what did we need them for? To hand out to our sewers and fabric suppliers?

Instead of printing letterhead and business cards, we invested in some great product photography and printed postcards that showcased our blankets and featured our website address in large font. These postcards served—and still serve—as one of our main marketing materials.

When starting out, it's a good idea to get what you can for free. We know lots of mompreneurs who launched their businesses by calling in favours. Jennifer Torres of Salsa Babies says, "A friend of my husband's printed my first flyers. A friend's brother did my website. Also, a good friend did my logo and all my branding—I pay her now, but initially she did it for me for free."

FROM THE MOUTHS OF MOMS

We have a lot of work done by friends or acquaintances—either on spec or for free. It's great, but it can also be slow because you can't hassle someone who is doing you a favour!

—Roz Heintzman, Mannerisms

The gals at Sweetpea Baby Food and Organic Snacks say they worked the "we're just starting out" angle to get deals on anything possible. The partners at Mabel's Labels had a very strict budget and committed to always try to get ten percent off. And some mompreneurs will get what they can for "contra"—in other words, they'll trade their product or service in exchange for the product or service they're after. Pretty smart, don't you think?

What you need to spend your money on depends on your particular business. If you're trying to accomplish a lot on a wing and a prayer, think about all the ways you can be creative about what you spend—or don't spend.

TIP: WHAT NOT TO SPEND MONEY ON IN THE EARLY DAYS

It's so easy to get caught up in the image of your new business. Over the years we've seen countless mompreneurs get wrapped up in the packaging of their companies. Spending money on things like printed shopping bags, lavish office space, and over-the-top websites is lots of fun but can be a real pain in your bottom . . . line. In your first year, spend your money to build infrastructure or generate revenue. If you do that, you'll be around for the pretty stuff later.

A successful male entrepreneur we know likes to think about spending in terms of "lasting power." Every dollar you don't spend on the things that aren't truly essential will allow you to stay in business just that much longer. Wouldn't you hate to have to close up shop before you really took off—just because of some silly spending in the beginning?

In life, we think that some things are more fun to spend money on than others. A new pair of shoes, for example, is kind of a fun way to spend money; a bikini wax is not—but it *is* necessary! So too in business are there fun purchases and less fun purchases.

We'd like to now chat about some of the less fun but necessary things you'll need to consider spending on. You may not enjoy parting with your money, but believe us, it'll be worth the investment. Here are our top three picks on where to spend your office and administrative dollars.

1. Invest in your legal status and your set-up

We're talking about setting up your business properly. This means registering your business, setting up business bank accounts, ordering company cheques, and getting yourself a company credit card. None of these things is even very costly—just a little time-consuming, and necessary, if you want to operate your business above board.

Talking to other people in business or researching online are good ways to figure out what kind of legal setup is best for you— and it doesn't have to cost you anything. What's more costly is when you need to call in the experts. We're talking about lawyers and accountants. If you need a partnership agreement or you plan on incorporating, you will incur one-time legal fees. The same goes for a non-compete agreement. It's expensive, but worth it. One mompreneur we know hired someone to do a job for her on a contract basis. When the contract was up, he went out and imitated her business concept completely. Here's what she had to say on the subject of upfront legalities: "In hindsight, I should have had a non-compete agreement with some key players. There are things I could have done at the outset to avoid problems down the road. If I had sought out professional advice I would have had the necessary protection."

You may not think that you have to spend the money on accountants and lawyers to set up your business. It will, however, cost you less to get started properly than to try to fix mistakes down the road. We just think it's best if you deal with these matters at the outset. Think about it like ripping off a Band-Aid: painful but necessary.

HOW MUCH IT COSTS TO SET YOURSELF UP IN BUSINESS

In most jurisdictions, you can incorporate online inexpensively (usually for about a couple of hundred dollars). You don't need a lawyer if you want to incorporate, although a lawyer may provide valuable advice. Talk to a lawyer if you draw up a legal contract (partnership agreement, franchise agreement, etc.), if you're leasing a property, or if you're buying a business. A lawyer will cost you approximately $200 to $500 per hour. All the information you need about incorporating can be found on the federal government's website, where you may also find an online database of accredited professionals, including lawyers and accountants.

—Prof. Reuber

2. Invest the time in your books and systems

Once upon a time, in the very early days of our business, one of us wanted to purchase some accounting software. But the other one didn't want to spend the money. She wanted to do our bookkeeping in Excel. (We *told* you we're cheap!) She thought we'd just keep a running spreadsheet of our sales and expenses. One of us won the argument and we purchased the software—the same software we use today actually. It has allowed us to enter thousands of sales each year and to keep track of everything we spend. It's how we calculate taxes payable. It stores information about our customers and what they've purchased in the past. It helps inform us about production issues and is key to much of our decision-making. We use it to mine data all the time. Not bad for $150.

If you can't—or won't—do your own bookkeeping, then you really ought to find someone who can help you with it. We would outsource it ourselves—we're just too cheap.

Last year, we were randomly selected for a government audit. (Gulp!) But it really helped that our files were sorted and our books were in relatively good order. Our accountant put the Government Lady in a room with our files and it ended up being no big deal. So when we say that you should take the time to set yourself up properly, we're hardly talking about anything extravagant—just take the time and spend the money to do it right.

On that note, you probably will need some kind of web presence. Today it seems like having a website is about as standard as having a telephone number. It's a quick and effective way for people to reach your company and learn what you're about. How big or fancy a website you have will depend on the kind of business you're running. Again, you don't have to knock yourself out. You may need nothing more than your logo and contact information up on the web. And anyone's teenage kid ought to be able to do that for you.

Remember, gals, we are as frugal as they come. As painful as it may seem to hand over all this cash at the beginning, we promise you, it will be worth it. If you spend now, you will save later.

3. Invest in your brand

A brand is a product (or service or concept) that's different from other products (or services or concepts), and that difference can be perceived by customers. Your brand communicates your unique offering in the marketplace.

Brands are often expressed in the form of logos (like the Nike swoosh or McDonald's golden arches). But your brand also includes some intangible qualities—it is the perception that people have of your company, and the way customers feel when they interact with you. Think about it. There's a reason you always reach for the Tide or Crest or Tampax despite the many options available. You have a relationship with the product that keeps you coming back. Over time, branding has become an increasingly important piece of the business equation, because that emotional connection between consumers and products translates into dollars.

Branding can be a fun and creative experience. Unsurprisingly, most mompreneurs we've met get really excited about this process.

You're bringing your baby to life in living colour. But you also get to choose if your baby is dressed in Old Navy or Juicy Couture. You'll have to set a budget for branding that's comfortable for you. (And even if she's wearing Old Navy, she can still look great.)

Devorah Miller, founder of children's clothing line Red Thread Design, understands how your brand can make your customers feel. She advises, "Carefully think out and invest in your brand— your look, your website, etc. It makes a huge difference in the way people interact with you."

Branding can be an ongoing process. Heck, even Apple changed its logo. But if you invest the time up front to think about what your company stands for, it will make a whole pile of decisions easier as you move forward.

If you have some seed money to get started and a vision of where you want to take your business, you should be able to come up with a budget that lets you sleep at night. Think about how much you need to spend to get where you want to go, and consider at what point you'll break-even on your investment. Sweet dreams. You'll be fine.

14

Playing well with others

Setting up supplier relationships

Maybe you've worked with suppliers in your professional life. Both of us did in our corporate jobs: graphic designers, printers, promotional goods specialists, event planners, travel agents—you name it. We worked for big name companies that used big name suppliers. Times were good and the spending was easy. And of course it was all on the company's dime.

Sourcing suppliers was an entirely different matter when it came time to develop our own product on a shoestring budget. It was shockingly hard to develop a good-looking baby blanket. We needed to open accounts with fabric and thread wholesalers. We needed to purchase sewing machines and sewing supplies. We needed to track down packing boxes and set up shipping contracts.

We quickly determined that we weren't going to get rich quick sewing blankets in our basement office. That meant we needed to find people who could cut, hem, and sew these blankets. We found ourselves in sweatshops—in downtown Toronto—where women sewed through the night after arriving from their day jobs. (This is not the production method we chose.) We dealt with a fabric wholesaler who called us "darling" and who we're pretty sure had an issue with non-prescription drugs. Many times in those early months we looked at one another and said, "They didn't teach us about this in business school."

When it comes to dealing with suppliers, we'd like to share with you some of the tips we've learned along the way, as well as some of the advice we received from mompreneurs.

Do your homework

In the olden days, we would thumb through the Yellow Pages to gather information, strengthening our biceps in the process. The Internet has made sourcing suppliers a whole lot easier—on our arms and our minds. Really, to find the suppliers that will help you develop your business, all you need to do is search online. All the information is right there.

Word of mouth may even be a better way to source suppliers. We recently had a lunch date with another mompreneur. Like us, her company works in textiles, but she manufactures a very different kind of product line. Nonetheless, we were able to swap lots of valuable information. By the time we'd polished off a plate of fries, we each had notes about the best travel websites, organic fabric suppliers, and international shipping options. Learning information from friends and colleagues is great because of the trust factor that you just don't get using the Internet alone. Word of mouth is like having the information pre-screened for you.

The rule of thumb when looking at potential suppliers is to get three quotes. This way you can make a fair judgment and decide with whom you'd like to work. You'll be able to compare prices, products, and personalities.

Here's a story a friend told us about a supplier experience:

"When we were planning to renovate our offices, we looked at three different contractors. One was so expensive that we would have had to remortgage our homes to pay the bill. The second contractor was quite expensive, but the guy was really fun and we got along great. We laughed during the introductory meeting, and we could see how much he enjoyed his work. The third supplier was a crusty pro who clearly knew his stuff, was cheap, but wasn't much fun. We went with Option 3. We shouldn't have. Pretty much since Day One, our personalities clashed. There were fights, grudges, and one telephone meeting that ended in a hang-up. And we needed this guy! We were knee-deep in the project and we felt like we were stuck with him. It's worth comparing suppliers based not on price alone. Make sure to find someone you can work with."

Now, we'd like to raise the point that it can be tricky to make some of these decisions on your own. As partners, we've had each other's back every step of the way. We check in with each other a gazillion times a day—even for the very smallest decisions. So when it comes time to choose the Biggies, having another person around can be really helpful.

Elizabeth Kaiden, founder of Two Rooms in New York City, started her business on her own. She had to make some high-stakes choices and quickly found herself in over her head. Elizabeth says, "Negotiating the lease, dealing with architects and contractors—everything was more expensive and took longer than I thought. I was inadequate to handle the task. My aunt is a real estate lawyer and I had another lawyer working for me pro bono. They advised me to have an 'out' clause in Year Three of my lease. If I didn't have that I'd have been in big trouble."

Thanks to the good advice from her aunt and lawyer, Elizabeth was able to avoid a potentially devastating situation. We strongly encourage you to have the right support in place—this can be anyone you trust—when it comes time to make your Big Decisions.

Tell your story

You might be surprised, but not everyone will be as excited to work with you as you are about working with them. In our experience, suppliers often think of small businesses as more trouble than they are worth—thorns in their sides. We, as small businesses, ask a lot of questions, demand good service, and expect to be treated well. Too much to ask? We don't think so. But don't be disappointed if your new supplier just isn't as jazzed about your new business as you are.

When we were starting out, we sat down with prospective suppliers and told them our plans for our business. We told them that we were in this for the long haul, and that we would make it worth their while to deal with us. (Lots of these operations are commission-based.) When we starting working with other mompreneur suppliers (like our graphic designer and our photographer), we told them that we wanted to grow with them—that working together would be good for everybody.

Earlier we mentioned working the "we're just starting out" angle. Well, Samantha Rosenberg, mom of a four-year-old boy and founder of online children's boutique Kitsel, did just this when she had to purchase inventory from a bunch of different suppliers. She says, "Some people were really mean and nasty and wouldn't be at all flexible on minimums." But Samantha persisted in telling her story and found that "some companies really believed in us and worked with us to help us get started."

It's worth telling your suppliers where you're coming from—and where you plan on going—so that they know what they can expect from you.

Ask and you shall receive . . . or not

You can ALWAYS ask for better pricing. You'll either get it or you won't, but it doesn't hurt to ask! Be aware that you're an unknown entity, so if at first you don't succeed, you can always ask again down the road. But do not assume that you're getting the best price when you're first starting out.

We set up an account with a fabric supplier who quoted us a price on fleece. We immediately asked if they could do any better on the pricing. Instantly, the price dropped $0.25 a metre. All we had to do was ask! We inquire about our pricing every year or so and have received subsequent discounts.

Also keep in mind that the more you buy, the better your pricing will be. So even if you're a small potatoes operation today, you might have more bargaining power in the future.

BENEFITS OF JOINING A PROFESSIONAL ASSOCIATION

It's worthwhile to consider joining a professional association related to your industry. This can be anything from your local chamber of commerce to a women's entrepreneur group. An association can provide support from a group of like-minded peers and resources from industry experts. Joining an association might also entitle you to better pricing on certain products and services. You might get a deal from preferred suppliers or enjoy better rates from financial institutions. Joining a professional association can also come with a hefty price tag, so you'll have to weigh the benefits of membership versus the cost to join. In making your decision, it's helpful to talk to other entrepreneurs about which associations they find the most valuable.

—Prof. Reuber

Find your fit

Sometimes two people just don't see eye-to-eye. This can happen with your suppliers. If your contact person isn't the right fit for you, try again. Hopefully you and your supplier will enjoy a long relationship together, so it's worth trying to work with someone there who understands you.

This happened to us with one of our key suppliers. A salesperson was assigned to us and she was, well, she was pretty ditzy. It was hard for us to work with her and we all wound up getting frustrated. We asked the manager if we could work with another salesperson and were accommodated. We've been happy working with this supplier ever since.

This reminds us of an experience we had at our hair salon. At this point, it should come as no surprise that we both have our hair cut by the same hairdresser. We liked the salon—we had been going there for years—but the haircuts had grown stale. We knew we had to break up with the hairdresser. It occurred to us to switch salons, but instead, we just switched hairdressers within the salon. Oh, it was awkward, but we're sure the salon is happy to still have our business, and we're happy with our new dos.

(As an aside, not long after we switched hairdressers, the salon posted a sign in the change room. The sign says something like, "Please feel free to try any of our stylists. We appreciate your patronage." Now, we don't know if that sign went up in our honour or not, but the point is they would rather have our business than not—even if it means switching things up.)

Be polite

We know, we know—it should go without saying—but being polite goes a long way. You can catch more flies with honey than vinegar, right? We know, you're the customer here and your suppliers should be happy to have your business. It's true. But you'll be working with these people for a long time. And you're just one customer to them, so if you can brighten their day, it'll probably pay off. And you're less likely to get screwed. That brings us to our final point about setting up your suppliers.

Invest in your relationships

Remember that banker we told you about when we talked about our business plan? He was good to us, so we thought that we should be good to him too. We sent him our company newsletters to tell him about what was going on at Admiral Road. We mailed him our press clippings to let him know about our accomplishments. Why wouldn't we? It didn't cost us anything. And if our banker felt like he had contributed to our success, we guessed that he would be there for us if we ever needed help again. And he was. Down the road he waived all kinds of bank fees. He also quickly put in place a short-term line of credit when we needed it.

Each Christmas we exhibit at a large and lovely craft show. As an exhibitor, we receive a handful of complimentary tickets to this pricey show. We'll share these tickets with our best customers, but we'll also put aside a few for key suppliers. We're guessing that you don't enjoy a ton of perks as a fabric salesperson, so getting a small freebie is kind of nice and always appreciated. Besides, we think it decreases the chances of our next fabric order going MIA before it hits the warehouse.

So let your suppliers know what you're up to. It doesn't cost much. And we can guarantee you that at one point or another, you'll need these people to do you a favour. There will be an emergency: you'll need something in a rush, or want something in a special way, or there will have been a miscommunication. Why not get your suppliers on your side? If you all feel like you're working for the same team, we promise that the sailing will be much smoother.

Ultimately, there is no mystery to setting up your supplier relationships. It's just people working with other people. Do your homework, ask questions, find people you like to work with, and treat them well. You'll hit the ground running in no time.

15

A work in progress

Developing your product or service

We've learned that raising kids is a long and sometimes expensive and difficult process. Hopefully the people we send out into the world as young adults have evolved significantly from their newborn states. In the same way, there is a difference between popping out your new baby business and seeing it as a full-fledged functioning entity out there in the world. We want to point out—whether you sell a product or offer a service—it might take some elbow grease before your offering is state of the art.

When we started our business, one of our goals was to sell something only if it was really beautiful. Today, we believe we have achieved that. But if we're telling you the truth, there are some baby blankets out there in the world that we sure wish didn't have our name on them. Some of those blankets in that first year just weren't as pretty as they are now. At the time, we were doing the best we could. But looking back, well, there was just a lot that we didn't know about how to get our product made. Where Admiral Road is today is quite different from where it was in its infancy.

So, what will be involved in raising your business? Lots of hard work, hustle, and probably a few freebies along the way.

Developing your product or service will be a process. It won't happen overnight. SavvyMom.ca co-founders Sarah Morgenstern and Minnow Hamilton talked extensively about their business idea while Sarah was still working full-time as a management consultant. When Sarah had her light bulb moment for their business, she sat down and wrote their first e-newsletter. It became the prototype for their business model. But even though they already had their "final product" in hand, they spent the better part of a year developing their concept, brand, and company. They didn't focus that much on the revenue during that time, rather they took that time to research, plan, and create their brand. It took time to develop the business.

Kathy Buckworth held various senior marketing positions before deciding to strike out on her own as a writer. About developing her offering, Kathy says, "I did a lot for free in the early days. I didn't get paid, but then it didn't cost me anything either. I learned that you can't only consider the money side of things. There are three things that I consider: am I learning something, am I deriving value, and am I making money at this? I want to know which side of that triangle I am hitting when I do something, and if that is what I need at that moment."

Kathy has tried a lot of different things in developing her offering. By hustling and seeing beyond the paycheque, she was able to find out what aspects of her offering worked best and were most desirable. Today Kathy is an award-winning writer, television personality, and public speaker. She recently released her fifth book—*Shut Up and Eat: Tales of Chicken, Children and Chardonnay.*

We'd now like to offer you some tips on how to develop your product or service in the early stages of your business to help get you to state of the art as quickly as possible.

Understand your target market

Your target market is the group of people you're trying to appeal to with your business offering. If you've written a business plan, you will have thought about who makes up your target market (remember Tracy?). Your target market doesn't include everyone in the whole wide world. Sad to say, but you just can't be everything to everyone all the time. (Hey, that sounds like motherhood!) Rather, your target market will be a group of a certain age, gender, economic status—or a combination of these groups.

Most often, the Admiral Road customer is a woman, aged thirty to forty, who orders online. Don't misunderstand us—we're delighted to sell a blanket to anyone of any age. But we don't focus our efforts on people who fall outside our core customer group because they represent only a small piece of the pie.

Understand who your customer is, and think about how to craft your offering so that your customer finds it appealing. If you don't know who your target market is, it's going to be really tricky to find them.

Set your pricing strategy

While you're developing your product or service, you'll need to spend time to set the appropriate pricing. How you set your price says something about your company—it reflects how you have positioned it in the market. Pricing your offering is trickier than you might think.

There are no absolute rules about pricing because what works best varies from situation to situation. However, we think there are three things you need to consider when figuring out if the price is right.

First, always cover your costs. Obviously you'll include the costs of making your product or delivering your service. But don't forget about your administrative overhead (rent, phone bill, Internet, etc.).

Second, consider the prices of the competition. It's going to be hard for you to sell your product or service for more than the going rate, no matter how fabulous it is.

Third, set the price as high as you can. It can be hard when you're first starting out to ask for the big bucks, but you'll soon find that you're worth it. Besides, no one is going to mind if you have to lower your price down the road. Give yourself some wiggle room for unforeseen pressures on your pricing in the future, such as a new competitor or innovation.

Get feedback from potential customers

When you're starting out, all feedback is valuable. You can always choose whether to take or leave someone's advice, but good ideas will often come from people who are slightly removed from your business.

One way to get some specific feedback on your offering is to hold a focus group. This means getting a bunch of people together in a room to ask them a pile of questions about your product or service. A focus group is a cheap way to gather a lot of information from people who are in your target market.

The mompreneurs at Sweetpea Baby Food and Organic Snacks held focus groups before launching their product. At the time, frozen organic baby food didn't exist. Since they were creating a new category in the market, they needed to find out a lot of information from potential customers. Would people be receptive to this kind of product? How much would they pay for it? Would babies like the taste? The Sweetpea founders made sure to ask people in their target market to participate in their focus groups. They asked themselves, "Who buys baby food?" Well, mostly moms. There was no point including baby boomers—men or women—in the focus groups, because they were never going to buy the product anyway.

Focus groups, even informal ones, are a great way to help you with specifics about your product, pricing, packaging—really, anything you can think of to ask.

Take it out for a spin

Not only do you have to develop your offering, but you would be well served to test it. Think about how you can get your wheels in motion before your "grand opening." This is sometimes called a "soft launch" and it's a great way to iron out the kinks before you've broadcast news of your new venture to the world.

If you can, start with your nearest and dearest. We have a mompreneur friend who asked us—and several other friends—to look at her beta website before she officially launched it. She relied on her friends to vet the website for content, spelling errors, and overall feel. This is a great risk-free way to tweak your offering since no "real" customers are checking it out yet.

You'll then want to hit some low-risk points of entry into the market. Businesses like retail stores and restaurants often quietly open their doors and begin operating for weeks before they officially announce their arrival on the scene. This allows you to get organized and familiar with the day-to-day needs of your business without attracting a ton of attention.

TIP: WORK FOR FRIENDS AND FAMILY FIRST

Some mompreneurs look to their immediate networks to get started. Graphic designer Mandy Webster did her first logos for friends and family. Founder of rock-it promotions Debra Goldblatt did her first big PR project for a friend. It worked for them and it can work for you too.

For us at Admiral Road, the main goal of our first year was to earn a spot at a big Christmas craft show. It's the largest, most prestigious show in the country, so we wanted to make sure we put our best foot forward. We knew of other vendors that had been rejected admission to the show, and we didn't want the same fate for ourselves. So we devised a plan to test our product. When Christmas came, we wanted to be ready.

Do you remember Tiffany? She was an 80s pop singer who scored big with her hit "I Think We're Alone Now." Tiffany launched her career by promoting herself in shopping malls across America. So did Admiral Road! Our very first show was in a shopping mall. Nobody knows that because about twelve people came to the show. But that was okay. It was our first attempt at merchandising—something we knew nothing about. It was our first chance to talk to real, live customers about our product. It was the first time we sold a blanket to someone who wasn't related to us.

Unlike Tiffany, we had only one experience in a shopping mall. But we did go on to do lots of other small shows. That first summer we were in business, we schlepped our wares all across southern Ontario. And we learned a ton. The small shows gave us a chance to interact with our customers, to see which products sold and which ones didn't, and to gauge reactions about pricing. The shows also taught us that sometimes a blanket doesn't just sell itself—we had to be salespeople! Since we didn't innately know how to do that, we had to learn.

Jennifer Salter, mom of three boys and owner of Lifeline Personal Training, laughs when she recalls how unprepared she was to meet her very first client. "I didn't even have a fitness plan for her," she says—something Jennifer wouldn't dream of today. But you have to start somewhere, and the only way you're going to learn is to jump in and test the waters.

Your first year is all about trial and error. Raising your business is just like raising your baby—you find out pretty quickly what it is you don't know. You might well end up adjusting your price, your product, or how you promote your offering. So let's keep going because this is a great time to talk about one of our favourite subjects—how to promote your business.

By the way, we were accepted into that big craft show in our first year. By the time the show rolled around, we were just a little more savvy and confident. We continue to exhibit there today and that show remains a cornerstone of our business. It's a place where we do great sales, reconnect with our customers, and try out new products. We also swap information with other crafters and always come away with a new insight or two. We have built our business on the back of that show, so it was well worth all the work we did in that first year to get there.

16

Getting the word out

How to market your business

We've already talked about how to price your offering, where to sell your offering, and how to develop it. So the next thing we need to turn our attention to is how you'll promote your new business.

You'll want to spend your marketing dollars on the things that are important in your industry. Does packaging make a difference to your product? How about the world's coolest website? If not, don't spend money on them. There are so many fun and innovative ways to market your offering. So before we talk about how to spend your marketing dollars, let's look at the things you can do for little or no money at all.

Marketing yourself on the cheap

In reading this book, you'll have noticed that one of our themes is how to get a lot done for a little. It's how we've done it—and it's been the same story for many mompreneurs we've met in our travels.

Social media

As we write, there is no bigger trend out there than social media—online sites that allow people to share information with each other (as opposed to traditional media like newspapers and television). Social media can take many forms, including networking websites, blogs, videos, and pictures.

From a small-business perspective, we think that the social media tools available are accessible and effective. And it's free. By posting information about your company on networking sites, you expose yourself to people with like-minded interests who may not otherwise find you. At Admiral Road we have blogged, Tweeted, and Facebooked. As a result, we have acquired plenty of new customers. There's really no limit to how you can promote yourself online—or how creative you can be. The use of social media for business is changing faster than Ashton Kutcher updates his Twitter page. For tips and ideas about putting social media to work for you, visit www.mominc.ca.

Co-marketing

Consider partnering with a complementary company to promote each other's offering. We've tried this with other mompreneur companies. It only costs us each a little, and the upside is great. In one instance, we worked with another business and each promoted the same contest on our blogs. The prize was a free personalized Admiral Road blanket and a product from the other company. To enter the contest, participants had to make a comment on our blog or the other company's blog. For just a little time and money, we were able to expose our customers to each other, generate a ton of positive content for our blogs, and at the end of the day, have one happy winner.

A website

Having a presence on the Internet to promote your business or ideas is imperative. Virtually everyone has access to a computer, so if you have anything to sell or anything to say, your customers can find out about it online. It doesn't have to be fancy and it doesn't have to cost a lot—it just needs to promote your company's message.

Testimonials

A testimonial is an endorsement of your product or service by someone outside your company. Once you've got your website up and running, ask a few of your customers or friends to write a testimonial. People really do look at all aspects of your website, and testimonials help to back up your offering. It's an easy and effective way to lend credibility to your company, so why not?

Publicity

Publicity refers to the process of generating buzz about your business. How fun does that sound? Everyone should get their company talked about (in a good way). Unlike advertising, where you pay to get your message out in a specific way (TV, radio, or print ads), with publicity you need only pay for the costs to get your message out to the media (by phone or email). The media then decide whether or not they want to pick up your story. One advantage of being written up in the media is that it gives you a level of credibility that advertising may not.

From where we sit, a focus on publicity has helped our growth tremendously. In our experience, publicity for Admiral Road is a direct driver of sales. If we can get our product in print, we see the impact immediately through orders coming in. Whenever we think about designing a new blanket or a new product, we keep in the back of our minds this question: Can we generate press around this? Heck, we've designed products just to get press! The impact can be that powerful.

Over the years, we've gone about trying to get publicity for Admiral Road in a variety of ways. Some ways have been (really) expensive, and some cost us nothing at all. We've hired publicists for five-figure projects, and we've also done the grunt work ourselves. Before we ever considered hiring a PR firm, we tried to promote Admiral Road to the media on our own. We enjoyed a decent amount of success: we had our blankets promoted on a local morning TV show, featured in a magazine, and showcased in national newspapers.

In fact, we were so buoyed by this success and what the media exposure did for our sales that we wanted to hire the pros to see how much more media we could garner. Not only did the PR firm help us land some plum media placements, we also learned a lot about dealing with the press.

PUBLIC RELATIONS AND WHAT A PR FIRM CAN DO FOR YOU

The good

There are three good reasons to hire a PR firm:

The firm can help you strategize about your offering and develop your "story." It'll also help you craft the key message you want to present to the media. It's great to have people outside your company hash out ideas— especially people who are experts in knowing what grabs the media's attention.

Schmoozing the media is what these people do, and their Rolodex probably has some names in it of people who you could only dream of getting in front of yourself.

There is a professional aura of someone acting on your behalf. The media can be honest with your publicist. And you avoid the feeling of being a door-to-door salesperson.

The good-to-know

With the right tools, you can act as your own publicity department. After going a few rounds with PR firms, we brought publicity back in-house. We had learned about the components of a press kit and we felt confident that we could go out and execute our publicity efforts ourselves.

We also learned that to grab the media's attention we needed an "angle." Now we can laugh at our first publicity effort. We wrote a press release and the headline was—wait for it—"Admiral Road turns one!" This, ladies, is not an angle. There's no clear message and no story. There's nothing for the media to grab onto. Later on, when we worked with professionals, we came up with some much more creative ideas. So if you're drafting your first press release, make sure to find a compelling angle. Talk about why your company is unique. Or what you're doing that's new. Or how your business solves a problem. Or how your business relates to a current trend. That's what the media will react to and deem newsworthy.

The bad

You don't have any control over how the media use your information or what any given media hit will do for your company. We have spent sleepless nights waiting for the newspaper to land on our doorsteps in the morning or anticipating a magazine issue hitting the stands. Until you see how your company has been treated by the media, you just won't know. We always wonder if the media will get our vital stats right (telephone number, website). Or worse, will we be portrayed negatively? One time, we got excited antici-pating exposure in a national magazine—the winter holiday issue, no less. Looking forward to some prime media real estate, we expected a slew of orders. But when the magazine arrived, we just shook our heads. Our blanket was in the background of a photo, buried in the crease of the magazine. The result was what Amy's husband deemed "a shade above useless."

For us, another downside of hiring a PR firm is the cost. You can hire a firm for a short-term project, but ideally, the firm will want to be kept on retainer for an extended period. That way, they can pitch your story when they hear of opportunities, instead of trying to ram your story down the media's throats over a short period of time that suits your schedule. Firms often charge thousands of dollars a month, making the cost prohibitive for many small businesses.

ADMIRAL ROAD'S FIVE-STEP PR RECIPE

Over time, we've watched and learned the formula for successful PR. There are never any guarantees when you undertake PR, but your odds will improve dramatically if you follow the formula. Below is our template for a successful PR campaign. (You can check out our website, www.mominc.ca, for more information about press kits, as well as a sample press release.)

1. Find something newsworthy to announce (e.g., new blanket styles, a charitable partnership).
2. Decide on the timing for your media coverage (know that magazines have a much longer lead time than newspapers, Internet, or TV).
3. Generate a media list (research the relevant contact person at your target newspaper, magazine, or TV show).
4. Develop a press kit (cover letter, press release, bio, company background, and, if applicable, product photography or a product sample).
5. Send and then follow up, follow up, follow up.

Sales promotions

Promotions are time-limited coupons, contests, or sales that provide ways to draw attention to your company, improve public awareness, and ultimately boost sales. You want to use sales promotions to increase demand for your product or service, so make sure that any offer you put out there is consistent with your company image.

One word of caution: if you have too many sales or coupons, your customers just may learn to never buy anything at full price. You probably want the sale to be the exception, not the rule.

Host a launch party

Once you throw open your doors for business, one thing you'll want to do is make sure that EVERYONE you know knows about it. One way to do this is to host a launch party. A few bottles of wine, some snacks, a debut of our product line, and an invitation to our family and friends is how we kicked things off at Admiral Road. Your launch doesn't need to be lavish. We hosted a party at home. And we didn't expect it, but we ended up selling product at our launch. (Enough to cover the cost of the party, in fact.) Maybe you want to consider giving your guests a "freebie"—a sample of your product or a coupon towards a future purchase. Remember that your nearest and dearest want to support you and they will be happy to celebrate your latest venture. So don't be shy—let your world know what you're up to.

A word about word of mouth

When we were talking about business planning, we mentioned the idea of word-of-mouth marketing. The process of passing information from person to person is widely considered to be an extremely valuable marketing tool. Good news travels fast, and bad news travels even faster.

Word of mouth is a fantastic and powerful marketing tool, so think of ways you can systematically increase it. (Becky suggests customer referrals, website testimonials, and participation in online communities.) It's great if you can create some buzz about your offering. Just keep in mind that you're going to have to plant the seed with a lot of people to make it work.

HOW BIG IS YOUR ADDRESS BOOK?

Over the years, we've been approached by many women wanting to start their own mompreneur businesses, many of whom are planning to rely heavily on word of mouth to launch their business. Unless you know seven thousand people, you might want to consider additional strategies. You're going to need a way to get those mouths talking before the word can spread.

Celebrity gifting

Years ago, we sent a handful of blankets to our favourite Hollywood moms. We thought that it would be great for business if we could get a celebrity mom photographed with one of our blankets. We heard back from a number of celebs and we were really pleased. And then one day, a beautiful handwritten note arrived in the mail. Julia Roberts wrote to tell us how much she loved the Admiral Road blankets we sent for her newborn twins. We slapped that note up on our website, and for years one of the main things that people knew about Admiral Road was that the Pretty Woman had our blankets.

Now, you can strike out on your own where celebrity gifting is concerned, or you can pay a gifting company for the opportunity to get your product into the hands of celebrities. With the right company, your odds of actually getting your product into celebrity hands can increase dramatically. On the other hand, it can be expensive and there are no guarantees that your business will grow as a result. If you're interested in spending your marketing dollars on celebrity gifting, consider your offering and think about what will happen *if* you get your product into the hands of a celebrity. It might be fun to see your earrings on the ears of the latest "It Girl," but you need to consider how you can turn that into an opportunity to sell more earrings. We're not going to lie—we think celebrity gifting is a blast—but we consider it more of a luxury than a necessity.

Do stuff for free

People *really* love getting things for free. One way to gain exposure for your company is to donate your product or service. We're routinely approached by not-for-profit organizations and schools looking to add our blankets to their raffles or silent auctions. If you think these communities are a good fit for your company, then you might consider donating something. You'll probably have your company name listed in a program and you might even find new customers.

Giveaways are another thing to consider. The blogging community is exploding and there are many blog review sites out there. How it typically works is that you send a sample of your product to a blogger and she posts a review of it on her site. For the cost of your product, you've essentially paid to advertise to that blogger's community. People are out there blogging about every topic under the sun, so you just need to find a blogging community that's relevant to your business.

Be creative

If your business starts out anything the way ours did, then you're looking at your sales force in the mirror. Selling was a skill we needed to learn on the fly, because they sure didn't teach us how to hawk a product in business school, and sometimes you'll need to get creative.

Sweetpea Baby Food and Organic Snacks is a company that got innovative about selling strategy. Their frozen organic baby food is sold nationally, but they don't have a big budget for marketing. Instead, they invented a selling strategy—what they call their ambassador program. Moms across the country promote Sweetpea at their baby groups, yoga classes, trade shows, and in-store demos. In exchange, the moms get paid in baby food. Since the company doesn't have an advertising budget, they get fans of their product to spread the word at the grassroots level.

Jennifer Salter of Lifeline Personal Training also found creative ways to send sales her way. After she launched her business, she connected with professionals in related fields, such as chiropractors and physiotherapists. Now she's got a roster of about twenty of these professionals who are a continual source of client referrals.

Charitable partnership

One way to get your name out there is to partner with a not-for-profit organization. A company will partner with an organization as a way to promote its brand, or to associate itself with a specific event or cause that relates to its brand, as well as to give back to the community. If you can find a good event or cause to hook up with, you might want to consider forming a charitable partnership.

For years Admiral Road teamed up with the African Wildlife Foundation (AWF). We donated a portion of proceeds from certain animal-themed blankets to the AWF, and in return, AWF promoted our company to their community. They also provided us with attractive cards we could enclose with our blankets letting people know that the gift they had received was doing some good. It was a great fit with our products and the young, animal-loving users of our blankets. We're currently teamed up with FreeSchools World Literacy and are supporting a women's sewing school in Delhi. We like the idea of mompreneurs helping other mompreneurs, and our customers do too.

We've loved our charitable relationships. Not only have we been able to cross-promote with the charities we've worked with, but it's given us a sense of personal satisfaction to have Admiral Road doing some good in the world.

Hustle

Not every business book is going to talk about the importance of hustle, but we're huge believers. It's good for business, and we can pretty much guarantee you it'll pay for itself. In Admiral Road's infancy, we did just about ANYTHING to make a sale. (Anything legal, that is.) At times that meant a special trip to the sewer across town to be able to ship out a blanket for the customer who needed it the next day, or getting in the car in a snowstorm to deliver blankets ourselves. We hustled our asses off. (Hey, it was helpful when trying to lose the baby weight.)

Now that our company is more mature and we have more systems in place, we feel like we can say no more confidently. It's not that we've lost our hustle, it's just that we now have a better sense of what's reasonable for our customers to expect and which things are worth it for us to do.

But starting out? Yeah—we hustled really hard. Did we do things that were unnecessary? Probably. But we were excited about what we were building and wanted to do our best. And we wouldn't have done it any other way.

Marketing yourself—investing in your growth

Sure, there are lots of great ways to spread the word about your company without dropping a lot of coin. But there are also important marketing techniques that'll cost you a little. You know how the saying goes: sometimes you have to spend money to make money.

Advertising

Advertising is a form of marketing in which you pay to promote your product or service. You might be talking about a small print ad in your kid's yearbook, or you might be talking about a commercial on TV. Radio ads, sponsoring an event, web banners—these are all forms of advertising. The goal of all advertising is the same: you want to promote your product or service and persuade someone to buy it.

Entire educational programs, books, and magazines are dedicated to the study of advertising. We just can't do the field justice here. If you want to learn more, there are tons of online resources out there. We can, however, share our own thoughts and experiences with advertising.

One issue we have with advertising is that you have to do it over and over again for it to be effective. You can't just run an ad once and expect to make your money back. Unfortunately, not many small businesses can keep up with the financial demands of ongoing advertising. Print ads in large magazines can run in the tens of thousands of dollars per issue. That can make for a pretty hefty customer conversion cost.

In our opinion, advertising is a "big fish" strategy. It can work well in combination with other marketing initiatives, or if you have the big budget to pursue it on an ongoing basis. We're not inclined to pay for advertising when there are so many other marketing strategies that we can pursue for free.

Trade shows

Oh, the trade show. Here we're talking about events organized so that companies in a certain industry can showcase their products and services. You've probably been to one—maybe for work or even a local home or hobby show. We have such a love-hate relationship with trade shows. On the one hand, we have built our business on the backs of them. Shows have been the most effective way for us to grow our business. On the other hand, there's the expense, the effort involved in setting up, the juggling of the child-care to work at the show, the waiting for the customers to come, and the tear down. Truth be told, trade shows are exhausting.

And you practically need a Ph.D. in mathematics to determine the formula of shows that are right for you. The sheer number of different kinds of trade shows out there is mind boggling.

Through a lot of experimentation, and yes, a lot of money flushed down the toilet, we've found the right approach to shows for Admiral Road. If we're being honest, we'd say that we've made some bad choices. We've made all the rookie mistakes: we've been reactionary, or we've gotten overly excited about a certain opportunity, or we've been motivated by the behaviour of our competition—sometimes all of the above. We've gone to shows and totally tanked out. I mean, really bombed.

But we will say one thing: We have *never* exhibited at a show and not learned something. Shows are a cauldron of information—from the customers you meet to the veteran at the next booth over to the show organizers themselves. If you're at a show and you're not busy selling, get busy asking questions. If we find that customers like something but won't commit to a purchase, we'll ask them, "What do you wish it had?" or "How much would you like it to cost?" It's a perfect opportunity to get information from the source. You've paid "rent" to be at the show, and we encourage you to make the most of your time there.

Shows are a popular way for new mompreneurs to get started, and we know lots of other businesses that market this way. We told you earlier about Samantha Linton's big investment to launch her soft-core porn video at a major sex show in Las Vegas. About the experience, Samantha says:

"We still ask ourselves if the trade show was worth the $15,000 that it cost. But it put us in touch directly with a major U.S. distributor. Furthermore, it was a different (and more positive) experience to be 'found' by the distributor as opposed to going home and chasing him on the phone for a meeting. While at the show, I also ran into an old colleague by chance and have since inked a deal with his cable company. I think that the exposure at the show just accelerated everything we were planning to do anyway. It would have taken us months to make the contacts that just came to us at the show."

Shows don't have to cost thousands of dollars. Churches, synagogues, and schools often host shows as fundraisers and charge only a nominal fee. If your business is suited to this kind of exposure, shows can be an excellent entry point into your market. At the very least, shows are a great place to learn a ton of information from exhibitors and customers alike.

TEN MARKETING TIPS FROM AN EXPERT

1. Be honest with yourself—an idea may look brilliant on paper but when executed may fall flat. Learn to move on.
2. Facts are your friends and numbers don't lie.
3. Never underestimate the value of customer service. It costs you nothing, but the returns are huge.
4. The more niche your marketing activities are, the better chance you have of striking a chord with the audience.
5. The more expensive your product or service is, the longer the decision-making process will be for your customer.
6. Keep things simple. If you can't describe your product or service in one sentence, how will your customer?
7. Small equals niche. You're not competing with the big guys; you're competing with the small guys.
8. Know who you are and what you do.
9. You're not always the target market for your product or service. Do your research on potential customers, not friends.

10. Marketing is a mix—you need to combine everything for the mix to work. Leaving out one ingredient will affect the mix and make another ingredient work harder.

—Debbi Arnold, DA Consulting

The kinds of marketing initiatives you pursue will depend on the kind of business you start. Given the number of mompreneurs we spoke to, we've met women who have tried it all. Some things worked and some didn't. Our message is that there's a lot you can do for a little.

We have found marketing our business fun and exciting and, best of all, worth the effort. As you can see, there are lots of ways to get the word out about your new business—now get out there and do it!

The Big Schmooze

Networking

We all have our own personal networks, but when you become a mompreneur, you'll likely have to seek out a new one. This might be very different from what you've experienced in the past. If you think about it, when you're in school, you have a built-in network of fellow students. When you work in an office, you have a built-in network of co-workers. And when you become a mom, all you have to do is walk to the park with your stroller to discover your new mommy network. Indeed, fear of loneliness is one reason women don't want to give mompreneurship a try. But becoming mompreneurs actually opened up a whole new network for us. Your network is out there—you'll just have to go out and find it.

Be open to opportunities

You never know what might come out of a networking opportunity, so be open to it. And there's no real downside other than the use of your time. One mompreneur suggests that "you should never turn down a meeting. You never know what opportunities can come from it. Also, if you ask someone for advice you should take it! You should really listen to what other people say."

As for us, we're keen to hear advice from anyone who wants to give it. It's free and chances are we'll get some food for thought. That being said, we've learned to trust our instincts above all. It's a lot like parenting—you know what's best for your baby.

Leverage your connections

You may not have a mompreneur network (yet), but you do have connections, so use them. One way to do this is to stay networked with your business and social past. Think about your Rolodex of Life. Call up former co-workers, camp friends, friends of friends, friends of your parents. In short, be in touch with everyone you can if there is even the slightest chance they can help you with your business (and even if they can't help you right now, keep them in mind for down the road).

The same but different

Other mompreneurs or competitors might feel threatened by you if they think you're honing in on their turf. Try reaching out to people who are selling in the same way as you, but who offer a different product or service. We're talking about networking at shows, lectures, and industry events. This means finding other business owners who share common ground, but perhaps not the same offering.

We've mentioned that we've learned a lot from talking to other exhibitors at shows. A jeweller, for example, isn't going to feel competitive with Admiral Road, but maybe she can recommend other good trade shows. We also swap information about suppliers with other mompreneur companies.

Take advantage of social media

We've touched on how to use social media tools to market your business. Facebook, Twitter, and LinkedIn are the holy trinity of social networking sites. Their raison d'être is to network. Getting online is an easy way to reach out to and join virtual communities.

We know of one story where social media brought two mompreneurs unexpectedly together. Nicole Morell at Honey-bunch.com writes a beautiful blog about her experience as a shop owner and mom of a four-year-old son and seven-year-old daughter. When another mompreneur found Nicole online, she reached out to her. Nicole says, "This woman who owns a baby boutique in Vermont read my blog and got in touch with me. Now we correspond all the time on business issues. Since we're not in competition with one another it works really well."

We've learned plenty from poking around on Facebook and Twitter. At no cost, social media tools are a low-risk way to find others out there like you.

Go outside your comfort zone (again!)

People like to talk about themselves—so even if you don't know the experts you want to reach, you can still call them up. The worst that can happen is they say no.

We honestly didn't have a clue about the publishing industry when we decided that we wanted to write a book. So what did we do? For starters, we remembered what saleswoman extraordinaire Hyla Pollak of Gemini Consulting told us over coffee a few years ago: "Ninety percent of what we want is outside our comfort zone—it's just a matter of being willing to take the step."

We sat down and thought of every person we knew who had

some connection to publishing and we reached out them. Our list included a friend who wrote a book about her experience as a lesbian parent, another friend-of-a-friend who wrote a cookbook, a friend of Amy's moms who used to work in children's book publishing (who we hadn't spoken to in twenty years), and a friend from elementary school working in publishing (who we also hadn't spoken to in twenty years). Each person we reached out to was extremely receptive. They gave us helpful tips too.

And then we did something that we never, ever do: we cold-called a customer from our Admiral Road database. We knew that she had been a magazine editor with a background in book publishing and we had heard great things about her. Because she had ordered blankets from us before, we knew she was familiar with Admiral Road. We had also sent her a press kit and blanket when pitching her magazine for PR. But we still thought it was pretty ballsy to call up this woman out of the blue to ask for her help with our project. (She, by the way, was completely extraordinary. She met with us on multiple occasions, dedicated hours of her time out of the kindness of her heart, made industry introductions for us, and basically is the reason we're able to write this book.)

We know one mompreneur who makes sure that she never leaves the house without her business cards. She has a game that she plays with herself: whenever she goes to a party, she forces herself to hand out at least one business card. Does she find it easy to do? Not necessarily—but it is how she's built her client base.

So if you get nervous before you make that phone call or send that email or introduce yourself, don't worry—it's probably because you're on to a good thing.

TEN TIPS FOR SUCCESSFUL NETWORKING

1. **Get an introduction.** If possible, see if anyone you know can introduce you to the contact you'd like to meet. It's easier to start an email with

"So-and-so suggested that I be in touch . . ." than to come at someone out of the blue. And from where we sit, if a colleague or a friend asks us as a favour to speak to someone they know who is just starting out, we never say no.

2. **Be straight up.** Tell the person you're reaching out to who you are and what you want from them. *Do not* call up a competitor and pretend to be someone else. You will get busted and you will burn bridges.

3. **Don't ask too much.** Be careful not to ask your contact for too much information. This person is doing you a favour. If you come in with a laundry list of questions, they will get burnt out or walk away with a bad feeling. Have a specific topic in mind that you'd like to discuss.

4. **Don't get too personal.** You'll make someone uncomfortable if you ask her about her sales numbers or how much money she earns. Of course you're curious! But a networking meeting is not the place to find out.

5. **Don't overstay your welcome.** Anyone will be happy to give you a half hour of her time. If you hit the one-hour mark, thank your contact for her time and ask if it would be okay to be back in touch at a later date if you have follow-up questions.

6. **Pay the bill for lunch.**

7. **Send a quick thank you** after the fact—it doesn't have to be fancy, a quick email will do. We've been known to Tweet a thank you too—it's a public expression of gratitude.

8. **Stay in touch.** If you see an article about something you think your contact would be interested in, then by all means send it along. It shows you're thinking of the person and is a great networking gesture. Or just call and say hello from time to time.

9. **Pay it forward.** Just as you are asking for help now, so too will newbies want help from you down the road. Be ready to do unto others as you would like done unto you. Besides, it's great to be the go-to girl—it only helps your reputation and will open up doors for you when the need arises.

10. **Practice!** If you're shy or reluctant to meet new people, then force

yourself, say, once a month, to make a new contact or reconnect with an old one. It'll only get easier.

Whether you're a networking natural or not, remember that it's free, business-enhancing, and always a good idea.

PART 5

BABY STEPS TO BIG STRIDES: MILESTONES AND HURDLES IN THE FIRST FIVE YEARS

Hitting the first birthday is cause for celebration. It's quite a trip, isn't it? The one-year mark provides a natural milestone at which you can stop and take a look around.

Just like a child, a one-year-old business is now a viable entity unto itself. Well, sort of. It's amazing to watch your one-year-old child tearing up the joint, but there is quite possibly no more dangerous creature on the planet—all of the ambition, and none of the sense. Just as a one-year-old child is mobile, your business too should be on the move. Whether it's crawling, walking, or running depends on a lot of factors, but one thing is for sure: it's not in the same place it was twelve months ago.

Your first birthday

Taking stock

How are things going in the business? One year in is the perfect time to ask yourself if you're on track with your goals. We are willing to bet that you didn't make as much money as you would have liked—it can be tricky to get the ball rolling in the first year, especially when juggling the competing demands of your family.

We've learned that you need some time to build momentum and achieve a critical mass of customers. For us it certainly didn't happen in Year 1 (or Year 2 either for that matter). But ask yourself, how did sales go? Did you break even? Make more? Or less? We also know that in the first year you're still investing in the building blocks of your business. You'll be buying things like software, office equipment, and lots more. This is where you pull your dusty business plan off your shelf and have a look at your financial projections. Have a look at your actual sales versus projected sales. Now do the same for costs.

If you haven't kept track of your finances, stop everything and get organized. You will never know where you're going if you don't know where you've been. We cannot stress enough how important it is to keep track of all the financials. If you don't feel like you're equipped for the job, then hire a bookkeeper. We promise you that well-organized financials will be worth the investment. We didn't truly get our books together until one year in, despite the fact that we'd set up systems from the get-go. We spent several weeks entering in the data from the previous year. It was an unpleasant task and a good lesson in keeping on top of the books. The biggest benefit though was creating a baseline for our sales, costs, and cash flow that we've referred to ever since.

TAX TRICK

How frequently you'll be required to remit sales tax depends on the amount you're remitting. Here's a trick that has helped us to stay on top of our book-keeping: in the early years, ask if you can remit your sales tax more often than is required. This way, you'll be obliged to get your books together more than just once a year. Eventually you will have to remit your tax frequently anyway, so it's a great habit to get into.

You'll find there is a lot to be learned by taking some time to analyze how well you did with both your sales and your spending. Odds are good that something will jump off the page at you and make you take action. You spent *how* much on bank fees? Time to call the banker and work out a better system. You only sold fifty percent of what you thought you'd sell of a certain product? Time to re-evaluate your offering or your marketing.

We like the story Samantha Rosenberg of Kitsel told us about the adjustments she needed to make to meet her goals. After starting her business she wasn't getting much traction with her new website and was quite distressed about it. She told us:

"For the first four or five months of my business, I went to bed every night and literally cried to my husband. I had borrowed $30,000 to start my business. I had built a website but had minimal sales. One night my husband turned to me and said, 'Stop crying. You've got this loan—so now find a way to make this business work.' He then asked me how many hours a day I was spending on my biz. I realized I was spending about an hour a day. The next day I got up and sent one hundred emails out to customers, vendors, and press."

In this example, Samantha changed her workload to meet her goals. Maybe a different mompreneur would simply change her goals to meet the time commitment she was willing to make. The key is to be evaluating all the time.

Thou shalt be flexible . . .

In the early days of your business, a little flexibility can go a long way. You never know what opportunities might present themselves. Mompreneur Debbi Arnold of DA Consulting experienced an evolution when she started her marketing consultancy. When she opened up shop she expected to be creating brochures and other corporate materials, but as it turned out there was demand for her services in creating marketing plans. As Debbi points out, "Your business may end up being dictated by your clients."

Anne-Sophie Falconer started her company, Lumiere Kids, by making beautiful lamp shades, until the owner of a hip children's store sent her down a different path. Today, she has a line of children's bedding, accessories, and clothes. She says, "Your first year is a good time to be flexible about your offering—you've got a little experience under your belt, but nothing is carved in stone."

THE IMPORTANCE OF EXPERIMENTATION IN YEAR 1

Few entrepreneurs have a perfect assessment of their market and their product right from the beginning. Yahoo! started out as a mechanism to manage research papers and Hotmail started out as an online personal database tool. But the founders of successful companies stay alert to where their companies are—and are not—gaining traction, and why. They're able to shift their attention to promising markets and offerings. For example, you may have started a personal concierge business aimed at providing services—such as dog walking, picking up dry cleaning, being there for deliveries, meal preparation, etc.—for busy couples living in the suburbs.

After operating for a few months, you may learn that much of your target market has children and someone in the house to care for them, so there is little demand for your services. Instead, there is a much greater interest from childless couples living in downtown condominiums, and they will pay handsomely for pet care services in particular. With the greater population density of condominiums, you can target a smaller geographic region to start, and can develop a suite of service offerings around pet care. This tactic lets you enter the market in a very focused way. You can learn how to serve this market well, build a reputation in this narrow niche, and leverage your knowledge and reputation to expand your service offerings or your geographic reach.

This flexibility—and the ability to shift gears quickly when required—is one of the key reasons that young and small firms can compete successfully against much larger and more established rivals. To be flexible, though, you need to minimize your investments early in your business. It would have been much harder for the entrepreneur described above to shift gears if she had invested heavily in suburban advertising, in partnerships with dry cleaners, and in kitchen facilities for meal preparation.

—Prof. Reuber

. . . but not reactive

Should you be flexible? Of course. But here comes the caveat. You'll want to avoid being reactive. In our experience, planning rather than reacting has been one of the hardest things to learn to do in business. We can't tell you how many times we've been going along, running our baby blanket business, when some "opportunity" comes along. All of a sudden we've dropped everything and are running the numbers of the next best thing. You'll be amazed at how many different triggers there are that can cause you to react. You hear about a cool new marketing opportunity (somehow these things are always time sensitive), a competitor is doing something different and you wonder if you should be doing it too, a customer requests something out of the ordinary—we could go on. The problem is that you can't always run the numbers (or you can, but it's probably just a stab in the dark), so you can go running off in a new direction with little information.

Yes, you need to be open to new ideas, and be flexible enough to make a change that will create value, but do keep your wits about you and have a rational plan for what you're doing. We can tell you that in our experience those time-sensitive, one-time "opportunities" are rarely what you think they will be. Take the time to make a plan, even a short-term one—it'll pay off.

The point is, one year in is a very good time to take stock. Odds are good that you didn't get everything right the first time around. And truth be told, you don't really know after a year if you're going to make it. But you can probably tell if you're moving in the wrong direction. By pulling up now, you can make the necessary adjustments to keep or start moving in the right direction.

So have a look at where you're at. Make sure you're on the right road and keep on trucking.

How are things with your family?

Beyond the money you've made, what were your other goals for your business this past year? How did you do with those? If part of your plan was to spend time with your kids, how did that end up?

As you head into your second year, you'll likely have begun to experience the true paradox of the mompreneur experience: although you started your business so that you could be more available to your family, as your business grows you're becoming less and less available to them. Suddenly you're shushing and delaying your children, not to mention anaesthetizing them with TV. Wait a minute—this wasn't the point! Better pack your bags, ladies, because it's time for the guilt trip. If you've got children older than a few weeks old, then you've come to know the unique hell that is Mommy Guilt. You know it when you see it—the feeling when you leave your toddler weeping at the preschool door so you can go and run your business. Or when your little one looks up at you with those big beautiful eyes and says, "Mommy, come and play with me," to which you avert *your* eyes and stammer something about a conference call in reply.

Mommy Guilt isn't unique to mompreneurs—any mother who attempts to do anything other than care for her children at all times will experience it. But there is something extra special about starting your very own business so you can be there with your children—only to not be able to be there.

Here's one story from our own Mommy Guilt experiences. When Danielle's oldest child was learning to count, he kept saying, "One, second, three, four . . ." Danielle couldn't figure it out. Then one day it dawned on her that he was so used to hearing Danielle say, "One second" in response to his queries that he figured that the word "one" is always followed by the word "second." As in,

"One second, honey, I'm coming." Or, "One second, sweetheart, I'll be right with you." Sigh. This is not Danielle's proudest parenting story, but it's God's honest truth, and unless you're a very strong and disciplined person, you've got your own special "one, second" story coming your way.

Every working mother finds her way to cope with the guilt. We're pretty sure that moms have felt guilty about all kinds of things since the beginning of time, but working-mom guilt is, we think, a paradox of modern motherhood. We're groomed and taught to be contributing (working) members of society. We learn the value of work. But somehow the old notions of what a "real" mother is have remained. We're supposed to want to be with our kids all the time, and we're *supposed* to feel bad about it if we want or need to do something else as well.

The mompreneurs we spoke to were philosophical about balancing work with motherhood and the inevitable guilt.

Lisa Will of Stonz says, "I've given up on the notion that the guilt will go away—it will always be there. But part of the guilt is that I really like my work. Even when I worked in my old job, I really loved my work life. I feel sad that my kids are growing up so fast, but I think I'd feel that same sadness even if I were at home with them full-time. I work a lot at night and go without sleep in order to spend more time with them during the day."

Here's what Victoria Turner of Pippalily and Simply on Board says: "At one time I would have looked at my daughter playing on her own and thought, 'I'm the worst mother in the world—I'm working and she's playing on her own.' Now I see that children benefit from independent play and from figuring out things on their own a bit. When I'm with my kids it's wonderful. It also makes me realize how much I appreciate having my work—having both." She sums it up beautifully by saying, "If someone says they have balance I'd really question it. There is no balance, only compromise."

Author Kathy Buckworth voiced her opinion on the topic: "It's hard to know when to be with the kids and when to be working. I think it's about setting up expectations. I may be at the hockey rink and working on my BlackBerry. My daughter might get angry if I missed her goal—but I'm clear that the only way I'm at the rink (or on the field trip, etc.) is because I'm going to need to get some work done at the same time. It's important to compartmentalize— but you have to make up your own compartments for work and family."

We love this piece of advice. Being a mompreneur requires making up some of your own rules. Your mompreneur experience is your own, so go ahead and make the compartments that work for you and don't think twice about what works for the mompreneur next door.

A number of the mompreneurs we spoke to learned about setting boundaries the hard way. One candid mompreneur had this to say: "I haven't been as invested in my family as I should have been. I'm trying to do it better now. I'm turning things away in favour of family time. We think if we don't answer the phone, meet the deadline, etc., it'll all fall apart. But your family will fall apart—there are consequences to not nurturing your family. You may need to drop balls in your business and you must accept that as a mompreneur. Otherwise we drop balls with our kids. It's easy to lose sight of why we did this in the first place. I wish I had taken time off with my kids, planned better. I've missed out on the youngest years of my kids. I didn't think I'd still be working so hard by now."

Mommy Guilt aside, your business has very likely made its presence known in your family's life. Whether you're doing takeout a few nights a week, have sourced some childcare, let the laundry pile up, or taken to locking yourself in the basement for hours on end— life is not what it would be had you decided to be a stay-at-home mom full-time. We think it's hugely important to remember that, as a mompreneur, you're neither a stay-at-home mom nor a career mom—so don't hold yourself to the same standards. (We're betting that even if you are a full-time straight-up mommy or a career mom, the standards women set for themselves are pretty much unreachable.) By embarking on mompreneurship, we're choosing something in the middle—so we need to be comfortable inhabiting that space.

When kids rear their cute little faces in the business

At the same time, odds are good that your family has shown its face within the confines of your business. If the kids start screaming every time you pick up the phone, you can't find your desk for the toys on it, and you find yourself being volunteered to help at every school function, you'll know what we mean.

We actually divided our roles based on the personalities of our children. Our first two children were born six months apart, and both were home with us full-time until about eighteen months. Amy's oldest, Jessie, had no interest in the car, which is a polite way of saying that she screamed every time she was put in it for more than ten minutes. Danielle's oldest, Charlie, actually seemed to like it. So, in the interest of the happiness of our children and our own sanity, we organized the business so that more car schlepping (and the half of the business that went with that) went to Danielle, while more stationary pursuits (and that half of the business) went to Amy. We ran things that way for more than five years before we made a change in the org chart.

Samantha Rosenberg of Kitsel has a hard time getting her little one to refrain from screaming every time the phone rings. She solved the problem by switching her correspondence to online. She has found that her suppliers and customers are usually perfectly happy to communicate via email, which suits her and her little guy just fine.

One of the—shall we say—"special" things about mompreneurship is your ability to double-dip into the well of insecurity. If you're anything like us, in the first year of both motherhood and business you can seriously doubt yourself. After all—what do any of us know if we've never done it before? Is it colic? Indigestion? Cash cycle problems? Who knows? But here's the good news: both of your babies will probably be just fine. The kid will stop crying, the bills will get paid. Of course, then the toddler years are upon you, and a whole new set of challenges awaits, but that's another story.

Ultimately, having your kids at home while you run your business is a bit like having your cake and eating it too. And you can. But only small bites at a time! So, if your kids are making their presence known in your business and it's not working for you, you may have to make a change to either your childcare arrangement or your working arrangement. Almost every mompreneur, especially those with small children at home, puts in long hours after bedtime. But we also know that if we choose to have the kids at home, then our working hours are going to be limited and our reserves of patience tested, at least until our children go to school.

On the plus side of working with kids around, lots of mompreneurs tell us that they feel they're setting a great example for their kids, especially their daughters. These moms tell us that their kids appreciate their mothers as working people, and see the value of hard work in following your dreams. In our experience, there's almost nothing nicer than hearing your child tell someone about your business. ("You know those blankets? *My* mom makes those blankets!") Or when your kid tells you that she'd like to work in your business with you when she grows up. So whenever the Mommy Guilt sneaks up on you, just remember that you're setting the ultimate example in hard work and determination.

We can tell you that the guilt does get easier as your kids get older and you get more established in your business. The first few years are a blur of work and kids, but over time you'll find yourself working differently, if not less. And your family will have grown into the new routine. Our kids understand that we have to work—it's a fact of life in our homes and it's rarely an issue anymore.

Mommy Guilt is inevitable for all working moms. All any of us can do is try our best to carve out time with our kids and actually be present with them when we do. And then we need to make peace with the guilt and get down to it when it's time to work.

How are your other relationships doing?

We know that the business can lead to Mommy Guilt, but what about your relationship with your husband? Nearly every mompreneur we talked to told us how amazingly supportive their husbands have been. In fact, we're willing to bet that most women who don't run businesses wouldn't believe what these husbands will do. One mompreneur tells us, "My husband has been so supportive. He would come home from working all day to a messy house and would sit down and fold laundry. He would tease me about when I would start making money, but I understood it because it has cost so much. I know that. I would book flights and hotels on my credit card when we didn't have the money. He's paid down my credit cards and debt so that I can do this."

But just because the husband of a mompreneur is a supportive guy doesn't mean there haven't been a few tense moments. Think about it—there the two of you are, humming along as a unit. Then you have a baby and this joyful but also incredibly time-consuming, attention-commanding, expensive person joins your household. Takes a little adjusting to, right? But then you add *another* time- and attention-consuming and even more expensive thing—your business—and the stress on the relationship is sure to mount.

Some of the mompreneurs we spoke to were very candid about the effects of their businesses on their marriages. One mompreneur (we're not naming names here) told us about the difficulties she faced. She was working long hours at getting her business off the ground. At the same time, she was frustrated by the demands on her at home in terms of childcare, housekeeping, and the rest of the "mom" jobs. This frantic gal found herself resenting her husband because she was working so much at her business and so much at home—she felt he didn't understand her workload. The good news is that the two of them underwent couples therapy to work through the problems and fortunately she now feels that her husband has a good understanding of the demands of her life.

FROM THE MOUTHS OF MOMS
I don't micromanage my husband. If he takes the kids to the dentist, I don't need to ask him about it. He'll tell me if there is anything I need to know.
—Victoria Sopik, Kids & Company

Another mompreneur told us her amazing story about the evolution of her husband's involvement in her business:

"My husband did not support the idea of my business—he thought it was a waste of time and money. I was supposed to be a stay-at-home mom, so why were we spending money for the kids to be in daycare? He couldn't see my long-term picture. I was afraid to share my dreams with him because he wasn't receptive. We weren't communicating well and we actually split up. Once he saw that I was treating it like a real business, he felt differently. We started to work on our marriage and have since gotten back together."

And a number of mompreneurs reported that their husbands felt resentful of their businesses in the early years when these burgeoning companies required so much attention. Before you call the guy all kinds of names, think about it from his perspective too. His wife, formerly at least a little available, is now MIA. More of the home and childcare has fallen into his lap. And all of this for a company that isn't even making much money yet! Now, hopefully your husband shares your vision for your business. (One of our husbands likes to say that he plans to retire on Admiral Road's earnings!) Or that he at least understands what it means to you. But if he's having trouble, take the time to really explain it to him and make him part of the excitement a new business can be. A number of the mompreneurs we spoke to had very involved partners, with mixed results.

We mentioned Candace Alper of Name Your Tune, who works closely with her husband, Eric. (Eric has a day job as a publicist but has been actively involved in her company since its inception.) Candace talks about the benefits of working with her spouse: "We get to see and appreciate each other professionally, which most couples don't get to do. We don't need to balance the parenting aspect since I'm at home, which helps. We've also had the opportunity to travel together for the business, which is great."

Another mompreneur had this to say about working closely with her life partner: "So many things in my business have been my husband pushing me, kicking and screaming all the way. Sometimes I resented it. Our relationship became about the business. It has been the ultimate of blood, sweat, and tears. There have been screaming matches and corks popping. They say that behind every great man is a great woman—but behind every mompreneur is a great husband."

We've also touched on the fact that some mompreneurs end up working with their husbands full-time. As the business grows, sometimes the most logical person to bring on board is the person who has had a good seat from the start. As we've mentioned before, many a mompreneur husband is effectively a silent partner from the get-go, so bringing him on as an active partner can make a lot of sense. With a little luck, a good deal of patience, and a whole lot of great communication, mompreneurs can make this work. Martha Scully of Canadian Sitter brought her husband into the business early on and they've now successfully worked together for years. Here's what she says about her experience: "Shortly after I launched my business, my husband quit his job and joined me. It was a little rocky at points in the beginning as we were developing the business. Now we have clearly defined roles that don't overlap. We talk about things but we each have our own workspace and our own jobs. We sometimes take separate vacations. Overall, it's been a really great thing for our relationship."

Involving your husband in the business can be a tricky thing despite the obvious perks. It's great to have the support and the extra set of hands, but on the other hand, how do you draw the line on what's yours to decide and what involves consensus? Most of the mompreneurs we spoke to who work closely with their husbands told us that the final say on a given issue goes to her. We think the key is to set the ground rules and have a clear set of expectations from the start.

We know some mompreneurs who feel sensitive about their husbands' involvement in their businesses. Does it make you less of an entrepreneur if you get a little help from your significant other? Of course not! We love how one mompreneur articulates the tension around this issue. She says, "I get sensitive about the idea that my husband has helped me to get my business off the ground. We're partners in all things—of course we help each other. It bothers me that people assume my husband has helped me. No one says that he is successful in his career because I make him dinner every night."

However you decide to work with—or not work with—your spouse, know that the business will be a factor in your relationship. In the best-case scenario, you'll both have a shared goal and a mutual source of pride, and in the worst-case scenario, you'll have a lot of talking to do to find yourselves on the same page. You can make it work—heck, if you're juggling a family and a business, you can do anything.

19

Is this what you had in mind?

How happy are you?

In the beginning of this section we talked about one year as being a good time to take stock of your business and make the necessary adjustments. But what about taking stock of yourself? Unless this wasn't your first swim in entrepreneurial waters, you likely had no idea what you were getting into. You started this business with a view to being a happy and productive person, right? So how are you doing?

Fingers crossed that at this point you're thrilled with your new life. Hopefully you've sorted out your schedule to find time for both work and family (with a little time for yourself in the mix). And hopefully your business is on its way and you're feeling content all around.

Now being the realistic gals we are, we're pretty sure that not *everything* is perfect in your life, no matter how much we can hope. Here are some of the themes that came up when we spoke to mompreneurs, along with some of their best tips for surviving as the chief bottle washer.

One of these moms is not like the others . . .

As you're rounding the lap into your second year of business, you may have noticed that you've set yourself apart from many of your peers. The fact that you're neither a career mom nor a stay-at-home mom means that mompreneurship can be a pretty lonely ride. If you've got a baby at home and are spending at least part of the day with her, you may find yourself at playgroups, in the park, etc., in the company of the warriors of motherhood known as the stay-at-home moms. These women are looking to occupy their kids and themselves throughout the day. They're in search of playdates and coffee dates. Of course they are—we'd do the same thing if we were with a baby all day long. After all, there's safety in numbers.

The problem is that you're not likely to be available for those activities. You're looking for any quiet few minutes to return phone calls, ship packages, or work on marketing initiatives. You don't have time for playdates! (This is where you worry that you're not providing enough stimulation to your children—the Mommy Guilt never rests!) Over time, you've probably found that while you're friendly with the stay-at-home moms, you're not really one of the gang.

Sara Bingham of WeeHands has experience with feeling out of the loop: "You don't quite fit in with the other moms. Your priorities are different. When I would drop off my kids at kindergarten the other moms would stand around and chat. I would run home to work for the two hours."

And Samantha Rosenberg had to make a change in some of her friendships in order to find a community: "The stay-at-home mom friends who had been amazing support through my son's medical problems didn't understand my business. They couldn't understand that I had to work. I wanted to tell them, 'I may not be setting the world on fire yet, but I have a plan and I will.' Some of them have never even been on my website. These days my closest friends also work from home—they get it."

On the other hand, the working moms who completely understand your need to get work done aren't really your peer group either. Since these moms have full-time care and are out of the house all day, it can be hard for them to relate to your part-time approach to work. If we're being really honest, we'd tell you that it's our sense that some of the working moms we know don't think we really work. It's true, we don't have to get up at the crack of dawn, kiss our babies goodbye, commute, take crap from idiot bosses, commute back, and *then* make dinner, do bath, and bed. We don't have to keep our kids up late (we're both fanatical about a 7:30 p.m. bedtime) because we've been with them during the day. And maybe we've been to baby music class during the day or taken the little one for a walk in the stroller. Of course to the career moms it *looks* like we don't work. We relate to mompreneur Melissa Arnott when she says, "I have a neighbour who likes to say, 'You've got the life.' People who are not really close to me will never get it."

So, here we are again, occupying that space in the middle. We're willing to bet that once you've got your business on its feet, you'll meet moms on both sides of the spectrum who will be downright envious of your ability to have a little of everything. Being in the middle is the whole point of being a mompreneur. We've always believed that you can't have everything in life, but being a mompreneur does give you a healthy amount of most of the things you want. A little Mommy and Me class? Sure. A little financial analysis? Yes! This may also mean a *little* money and a *little* time for yourself—but that's part of the deal.

Despite the obvious attractions of the mompreneur lifestyle, many mompreneurs report that it can be a solitary space to inhabit. This is particularly true for sole proprietors. Sure, starting a business is exhilarating, but putting in hours on end alone at home can be isolating. Of course it depends on your personality and whether you're suited to putting in time on your own, and also how social the nature of your business is. Some mompreneurs rarely experience loneliness, but overwhelmingly we heard that it's part of the mompreneurship experience. It's hard to appreciate how difficult it can be to go it alone for months or years on end before you find yourself there. One of our mompreneur friends closed the retail store she had run for several years and changed her model to a home-based business. Here's what she has to say about the loneliness factor: "Now that I work from home, I'm struggling with the isolation. I fear that it's affecting my decision-making. It's a worse problem than I had anticipated."

FIVE WAYS TO COMBAT THE SOCIAL SIBERIA OF SELF-EMPLOYMENT
1. Talk to other mompreneurs
2. Get online—blog or tweet—and join the conversation
3. Join a business networking group
4. Go to the gym
5. Meet a friend or colleague for lunch

And lots of mompreneurs just don't worry about where they fit in. Jennifer Torres of Salsa Babies puts it this way: "I love where I am. I don't engage in the fight between career and stay-at-home mom. I'm pretty confident in who I am and what's important to me. I'd never knock being a stay-at-home mom—my mom was one and she was great at it. Also, it's way harder! On the other hand, at a party it's nice to be able to talk about my work and have people be interested. I used to think that if I won the lottery I'd be a stay-at-home mom. Now I think I'd still work. I see what it gives me—I love the creative and the social aspects. It's kind of my Me Time. I also love what it's done for my daughters. They are developing their own entrepreneurial spirits."

Author and TV personality Kathy Buckworth also likes where she is: "I like being in the middle. I don't have time to compete with other women—I like to talk to my old friends from the corporate world (in part it reminds me why I do what I do) and I like to talk to the stay-at-home moms."

As for us, we're not going to pretend that we're not aware of our lack of social action. Ultimately though, we both love working from home and are comfortable with our own company. Sure, the company Christmas party means going to a hotel for tea for two, and a corporate "retreat" means dragging ourselves and our wares to an outdoor show—but it's the choice we've made and we're happy with. Neither of us can imagine being willing to give up the comforts of the home office and the flexible schedule for any other life.

At the end of the day, the fact that your life will look different from that of your peers is not only surmountable but also something you can embrace. While it's important to be aware of the possibility for isolation and loneliness, there are strategies for dealing with it that are at your fingertips. Not only will your business survive if you take some time to get out and talk to other grown-ups, you'll be re-energized, refreshed, and a better mom and businessperson for it.

Staying motivated in the business

It's true that entrepreneurs don't get performance reviews or promotions. It can be hard to gauge your success. Hopefully your success is showing on the bottom line. But even if it's not, don't forget to come back to your list of reasons for starting the business in the first place. It's easy to get caught up in noticing what everyone else is doing and to focus on all that you're not. We're willing to bet that if you can take a look at your accomplishments as a whole (entrepreneur, mother, partner, friend, etc.), you'll be amazed at what you've done.

There are always opportunities for feedback. Kathy Buckworth suggests that mompreneurs make an effort by entering contests and getting themselves nominated for awards. She says, "As a mompreneur you only get feedback from your kids, and they always tell you that you suck! You have to get outside recognition and validation when you can. Enter contests—even if you don't win, you'll often get good feedback."

We love this advice. We've found that putting ourselves "out there" for media has also helped us articulate our story and has made us look at our company as an outsider would. It's a great exercise.

Even if you have no issue with self-motivation, external validation is always nice. We love to collect testimonials and photos of adorable babies using our products. Every time someone sends us a photo of their baby with one of our blankets, it's like a little present. And when one of us is feeling a little blah about the business, the other one is sure to remind her how many of our goals we're meeting. We make sure to celebrate all of our accomplishments, even if it's just the two of us.

Separating the business from the rest of your life

For the mompreneur, the lines between work and family life can get pretty fuzzy. This is especially true if you work from home. As we've said before, lots of mompreneurs swear that you can't run your business and do laundry at the same time. Now, we happen to love that we *could* do the laundry while working. We don't (laundry happens after hours), but we love that we could!

For lots of mompreneurs, the lack of separation between work and the rest of your life can be troublesome. Remember when you were a student and there was always something you could be doing? There was always a book to read or a paper or project you should be working on, right? Well, that's life for the mompreneur. The idea of the mompreneur who doesn't have something in her business that needs doing is surely an urban myth.

If you work from home it's easy to never stop working, or on the flip side, to never really focus on your work because there are kids and pets to feed, messes to be cleaned up, a ringing phone, the neighbour dropping in for coffee, etc. Many mompreneurs find it helpful to find ways to delineate work time from the rest of their lives.

TIP: HOW TO WORK FROM HOME AND ACTUALLY GET THE WORK DONE

1. **Get "dressed" for work:** we all know that we're more productive when we feel more professional. It's hard to feel like a powerhouse when you're in your PJs.
2. **Walk to work:** some mompreneurs take themselves for a walk around the block before work if they work from home—it helps them delineate their work time.
3. **Come up with (and stick to!) office hours:** some mompreneurs even post the hours on the door to their office to make it clear to the rest of the family.

4. **Come up with (and stick to!) home/life hours:** designate time during the week to get a haircut, see the dentist, get a pedi, call a friend, whatever. If you worked outside the house you'd find time to get these things done, so make sure to find time if you work from a home office as well.
5. **Have a separate workspace:** ideally you can close the door at the end of the day. It's helpful when you can "finish" work and walk away.

Work at home versus housework

And as for that laundry, lots of mompreneurs just don't do it during their workday. This is confusing to some husbands. Carol Pitre of Kid Brother Clothing, a line of clothing for boys, and mom of three, tells us that her husband can't understand why she can't do laundry while working. We laughed when she reported telling him, "I'm working *in* the home, not *on* the home!"

Other women have let some of the expectations around housework go in the name of their sanity. Jo Saul, who owns Type bookstores in Toronto, tells us, "I don't have any help at home. At 5:30 I pick up the kids and it's a mad rush to the end of the day. The breakfast dishes are still in the sink when I get home." Stacey Helpert, an event planner and mom of three, shares the issue of the mess: "I'm super organized at work—but my house is a disaster because I'm not solely in control . . . my kids are!"

What about getting some help with it all? That's what some women we know have done. Jennifer Torres tells us, "I finally broke down and got a cleaning lady, once a month. And an accountant. . You can't do it all."

Taking care of You

How happy you are in your business has a lot to do with how happy and healthy you are in your life overall. If you're burnt out and stressed out, you're going to want to bail on your business a whole lot sooner than if you are at least a little sane. This would apply to anyone in any job, of course. (We know a woman who took a medical leave from her corporate job for "situational sadness." The situation causing the sadness happened to be her crappy job.) The only difference is that you have some control over your schedule as a mompreneur, so go ahead and take it.

Take care of yourself physically. What they say about exercise giving you more energy is absolutely true. Exercise with a friend so you can also socialize, or do something active with your kids so you can spend some time with them. If you can kill a couple of birds with one stone, all the better.

See friends, see a movie, do what you love. At least sometimes. We promise it'll more than pay for itself. The time you take back from your family and business will replenish you and make you better all around. After all, you're the boss of you—so be a good one.

At the end of the day—you know how the song goes—if you're happy and you know it, clap your hands. If you're not—it's time to take stock and see what changes you can make to make it work.

20

Stop the ride, I want off

When to call it quits

Okay, here's the bad news: most small businesses fail. Believe us, this is not what we want to be talking about in a book about how to be the best mompreneur you can be—but it's the truth and we've got to get down to it. There are varying sources on the statistics around new businesses, but on average the research suggests that about fifty percent of small businesses fail within the first year, and ninety percent within the first five years. Sobering, isn't it?

We've noticed, however, that mompreneurs seem to outlast the statistics. We suspect that since many mompreneurs aren't on the hook for supporting their families with their businesses, the stakes are lower and the business can afford to grow more slowly than, say, a venture on which you depend to feed your kids. Truth be told, if we had needed to feed our kids and pay the mortgage in the early years, we'd definitely be one of the statistics.

There aren't a lot of hard data about the success rate of mompreneur businesses, but we do know that two-thirds of all female entrepreneurs rely on a source of income outside of what they derive from their business. On the plus side, we've got the ability to give our businesses the time and space they need to grow, but conversely, if you're not in it for the money it may be hard to know when to quit.

We've been watching other mompreneurs for years now, but only occasionally have we seen one pack it in outright. Many women invest a nominal amount of money when they start up, and work part-time. As we've pointed out, it's hard to expect huge returns for small investments of time and capital. So it's not hard to imagine how a mompreneur could tolerate minimal returns for a few years, or longer.

It may be that you look up one day and realize that you're not making enough money to justify the demands. Maybe changes in the industry or market have created seemingly insurmountable challenges.

Or it may be that running your own business isn't jiving with the rest of your life at the moment. Many of the mompreneurs we spoke to had faced real challenges in their family lives—infertility, illness (their own and their children), marital strife, and more. No matter how hard we try, we aren't going to be able to control everything in our lives. No matter how hard we work to carve out time for family, work, and ourselves, sometimes life is going to throw us a curveball.

Of course you may not be measuring what you "invest" and what you "lose" in terms of money, but rather in terms of time and energy. What constitutes whether your business is "working out" is personal to you, but we strongly encourage you to be honest about it. This is where having your goals clearly laid out becomes very important. You need to have something against which to measure your success.

WHEN TO LET YOUR BUSINESS GO

"Underperforming" is of course a subjective assessment, and depends on your objectives. What might be an adequate financial return for one person may be too low for someone else.

It can be tricky to know when your business is no longer viable. Those who are closest to you may protect you from the truth. Your employees will have a vested interest in your continuing to operate, as will your customers who rely on what you sell and your suppliers who rely on what you buy. It's impossible to provide general guidelines for when you should throw in the towel, but if you're losing customers or your customer base is stagnant at a level that's not profitable, it is certainly time.

It's common for entrepreneurs to hold on too long to businesses that are not financially viable. Some don't want to let their business go because they have invested so much time, effort, and money into it. Others are afraid of losing face to their family or community. People who have more options are more apt to let go easily. If you're thinking about closing your business, it's worthwhile to think about the experience you've gained in starting and running it. Your resumé looks very different now and it's valuable to think about how you can capitalize on this, either in the job market or in starting another company.

—Prof. Reuber

Now, of course we would encourage you to find a way to get over the hurdles in front of you and continue to work at your business. But we also recognize that sometimes it's just not working, or the price you're paying for your business in the other areas of your life is just not worth it.

The decision to close up shop can be agonizing, no matter how sure you are of the underlying reasoning. We've learned that one's business is an incredibly personal thing. It's like another baby in your life. It's easy to feel that your business is simply an extension of yourself. No one wants to stand up and tell the world that the venture they invested their blood, sweat, and tears in just didn't pan out. So to admit failure can be unappealing in the best case and devastating in the worst case. But here's where the parallels between raising your kids and your business end: you'd never desert your kids when the going gets tough—but you can close your business and live to tell the tale.

Elizabeth Kaiden experienced the anguish of closing up shop:

"My business died in its infancy at one year old. Financially, my business was a disaster. We were making plans to shut down. I was pushing my third child in the stroller to what was to have been our penultimate board meeting. I couldn't do it. I turned the stroller around and went home. We closed our doors a few weeks later. I consider my business to be a failure and failure is painful. Looking back I realize that I was depressed for a full year after my business failed. I fantasized ceaselessly about restarting it. I'm not necessarily glad I started the business."

We want to talk about this issue not to scare you but to let you know that some of us are going to fail the first time around. And to let you know that it's not the end of the world. Every mompreneur we know who has failed in her business has made it through to the other side in her life.

So how do you bow out gracefully? Well, there are a few ways out.

Sell your business

If you want out but believe there are assets worth having in your company, why not see if you can sell the business. (Of course you can also sell it because you're wildly successful and are ready to move on to the next venture!) We told you how we bought our business from a woman who no longer had the means or the interest to run it. She certainly didn't get rich off the deal—but she did unload some equipment and inventory and made a few dollars for her troubles. Depending on the health and viability of your business, you might just make some good money for your efforts. If you're planning to sell, consult a lawyer or banker to help you determine the appropriate value.

Just as you make repairs and improvements before putting your house on the market, you should make your business as attractive as possible to potential buyers:

1. Make sure your accounting records are up-to-date so prospective buyers can make a proper valuation.
2. Have a customer database so prospective buyers understand your market.
3. Prospective buyers will check you out carefully, so disclose anything that could be a nasty surprise for them (e.g., an ongoing lawsuit, taxes in arrears, or an employee's human rights grievance).
4. The price you get for your business will be determined by the profits the new owner expects to make, so sell when the business is strong. You will get more when the company is growing than when it has reached its peak.
5. Identify your intellectual property (any patents or trademarks, etc.) and show how you have protected them.

—Prof. Reuber

Reinvent your business

If your business isn't making ends meet, why not consider changing the format? If you've got physical space and staff, you can always downsize and work from home. Paula Jubinville's business was very successful, but changes in the personal lives of both partners led to the decision to scale down:

"We got to be quite big—we had multiple offices. I was running the business more than dealing with clients. After about five years our life plans changed. We had promised ourselves that the business would never dictate the way we wanted to live our lives. Around the time I was thinking about children, my business partner wanted to move across the country. Our leases were also ending. I hand-picked the clients to bring with me when I went out on my own. We kept the remaining clients with the associates who had been servicing them. It kept things consistent for the clients and also gave our employees a head start going out on their own. It was a matter of choice. I didn't feel like it was something that was happening to me. I was proud of what we had accomplished. I moved back to my home office and my partner moved away. Her moving was heartbreaking—that was the only sad part."

If downsizing and working at home doesn't work for you, you could also consider freelancing in-house for another company. That way you can do your thing and ultimately control your destiny, but at the same time you've got the camaraderie, paycheque, and structure that a workplace provides.

Wading back into the workplace

Whether you need the cash or just a change of pace, returning to work for a while can actually be just what the doctor ordered. The mompreneurs we spoke to who went back to working for someone else after their businesses wound down told us that the regular paycheque and ability to turn off at the end of the day were refreshing.

Regrouping and starting again

What struck us in our conversations with mompreneurs who had experienced a business failure was that they all wanted another kick at the can. Somehow it seems that whatever mistakes they made, they felt re-energized and ready to apply what they learned to a new venture. Jordan Maher put it this way:

"At the time, I knew the business was dying. I didn't want to stay home and think about it. I went back to work part-time. I understood all the ways I'd gone wrong—I had learned so much about business, PR, my customers—everything I should have known at the start. Then my husband had an accident (he's fine now) and all of my priorities were reshuffled. I knew I had to stop. I cancelled the last of my scheduled programs and then very quietly shut the doors. There was no announcement or anything. At the time it was easy—I didn't feel like I had a choice, and I had no time to think about it. Now I miss the idea of having something beyond my family. These days I'm developing new ideas—and starting with a business plan!"

It just goes to show that if at first you don't succeed . . . there's a great new venture around the corner. Alison Smith took what she learned from her first business and did big things with it in her new venture, EchoAge. Alison says, "With my first company, I saw a need in the market, but it was about my design sensibility—it was very personal. Even though EchoAge is a totally different business, there is lots of crossover. Everything that I've done has built on other things, giving me a bank of experience: I know what my work ethic is; I'm not afraid of work that needs to get done; I learned skills in my corporate background and also as a mother. Now I can put it all together."

We spend a lot of time thinking about other small businesses. We know of a couple of amazing companies that seemed to jettison out of the gate. They seemed successful almost overnight and this perplexed us. Then we found out that these entrepreneurs weren't on their first try. There's a lot to be learned from a business failing—and there are some terrific entrepreneurs with amazing companies who are benefiting from earlier learning.

Of course no one sets out to fail at her business. On the contrary, we pour every ounce of ourselves into it. But there's pride to be found in just doing it. We love how Elizabeth Kaiden sums up her entrepreneurial experience: "I just did it. I climbed Mount Everest even though I was totally unprepared for it. I did something idiotic, risky, and potentially harmful to my family. Parenting makes you cautious—with good reason—but that's not something I ever wanted to be. But I proved that I'm still me—even as a parent."

Whether you close the doors forever and move onto new opportunities, or whether you've become a serial mompreneur and move on to new businesses, either way you'll have learned a lot about business and yourself along the way. Wherever you get to, it's an amazing trip.

And as for taking the setback personally, mom and bookstore owner Jo Saul puts it best when she says, "Your business is not you." If you've made the choice to pack it in, know that you've done more than most people ever do in trying. And you've done the mompreneur sisterhood proud.

21

Up and running

How your business is developing in the early years

If you've been a mompreneur for a few years, then you'll have some idea of what you're dealing with—professionally and personally. You understand what is required to run your business and your home life on a day-to-day basis.

At this stage, you also know what you want. It doesn't matter if you're motivated by financial success or the thought of seeing the hot UPS guy on his afternoon pickup route, but you should be clear on your goals. (And if you're not clear on your goals, check in with yourself again. This is too hard to do without knowing why you're doing it.)

In our case, we also learned who we were: we knew what Admiral Road was (and wasn't), and we knew how much we wanted to be involved in our children's lives. We had a sense of what was required to run our business and our families.

By this time in our business, we had figured out how to make and market our product. We began to outsource parts of production and administration so that we could concentrate on growth. We expanded our product line and streamlined our pricing. We raised our prices to accommodate increased costs. It was a time of great personal learning. Our business was ticking along but our "to do" list was unending. We revisited our financial goals and improved our supplier relationships. We divided our job responsibilities. We revised our marketing plan constantly. We also attracted enough attention to be imitated and had to deal with the frustration surrounding that.

Our children were coming along too. They started daycare and preschool. There were playdates and birthday parties and more pregnancies. (We used to joke that it wouldn't be a trade show setup unless one of us was pregnant. And then we'd be grateful that we sold baby blankets and not anvils!)

PUT DOWN THE TAPE GUN

By now you're probably busy enough that you've got lots and lots to do. It's time to ask yourself if what you're doing is a revenue-generating activity. Are you spending days shipping out boxes? Doing data entry? There are other people who can do that for you—but only you can determine the strategic direction of your company. Shell out a few bucks and free yourself from the minutiae so you can focus on the bigger picture.

Many small-business owners eventually realize that just as they had to learn how to get their venture off the ground, they now have to learn new skills to take it to the next level.

Broadly speaking, there are two things we need to think about—first, how to grow, and second, how to manage that growth. But first, let's take a moment to assess where you're at in the toddler years of your business.

You know how school report cards have categories like "meets expectations"? We're going to borrow a page from the local school board and look at measuring where you're at on the growth chart of your business.

Developing below expected level

Not everything always goes according to plan. There's a term pediatricians use when things aren't going well with your kid—"failure to thrive." These are words no mom likes to hear. If this is the case with your business then you'll need to take a good, hard look at where you're at and where you're going. (Unlike being a mother, you have the prerogative to quit your business.) You might need to readjust your sales goals to reflect other realities in your life.

It's interesting to note, however, the tremendous optimism from the mompreneurs we've met—even if they haven't hit their sales targets. One woman we met describes her experience as a mompreneur like this: "It's been a constant emotional roller coaster of ups and downs. I don't think people realize how much work it is and how much disappointment there is. You just have to keep working hard, plugging away. I'm still struggling along, not making any money. I've invested in my brand, press, and product. I'm still looking at the bigger picture."

In some ways, we suppose it's how you define your business's development. For many mompreneurs, it doesn't always translate to the bottom line. One mompreneur tells us, "I'm not making as much money as I thought, but that doesn't mean much. I'm growing like crazy."

A common refrain from mompreneurs is that "getting there" has, like most things, taken twice as long and cost twice as much and been twice as hard as they expected. Our advice is to just keep checking in with yourself. If things haven't unfolded exactly the way you thought they would, ask yourself if you're still enjoying the business. Are you headed in the right direction? Are your kids okay? Your husband? Maybe you need to revise your timelines or your goals. Try this exercise: Even if your business isn't where you thought it would be, go through your personal checklist. If you can still check off more pros than cons for being in business for yourself, then forge ahead.

Developing at expected level

In this scenario, your business is developing just like you thought it would. One mompreneur tells us, "I've never run a deficit, but I've never made that much profit either." If you've been humming along, maybe it's time to think about where you can take the business from here and how you can improve on current processes and systems. If everything has gone according to plan, then raise the bar. See what target you can hit or what goal you can check off next.

Developing above expected level

Many mompreneurs impressed us—and themselves—with what they've been able to accomplish. They have grown faster and made more money than they ever expected.

We spoke to Victoria Turner of Pippalily and Simply on Board, who says, "I've grown so much for a long time. I'm doing far better than I would have thought."

Graphic designer Mandy Webster has also exceeded her own expectations for her business. The reason that things have gone so well—one great client—is also a risk in her service-based business. Mandy points out, "I make more than I thought I would. I had low expectations and it's gone well. One problem is that I've had a great client for the past few years—it's been my bread and butter—and I've become complacent. My contact there has now been promoted and the work is less sure. I'm not sure how well I'll do this year."

Now is a great time to figure out on which side your bread is buttered. Look at how you can nurture existing customer relationships. Even more importantly, think about where you'll find new customers and what you'll need to do to get them.

The Big Break

It doesn't matter how small a business you start—we have yet to meet a mompreneur who doesn't dream about catching the Big Break. It's the same kind of fantasy we all have about winning the lottery. We know our chances aren't good, but someone has to win. It might as well be us, right?

We all want to get on *Oprah*, or receive the order from Target, or appear in the pages of *InStyle* magazine. But are these dreams all that they're cracked up to be?

To be sure, we know of mompreneurs who have been on Oprah or have gotten the call from Target, and their businesses have been catapulted into the stratosphere. But sometimes the Big Break isn't the answer to all your prayers.

The Big Break: Our story

Now we're going to tell you a painful story. Danielle actually refers to it as the lowest point in Admiral Road history.

We had been in business for three years when we decided that we wanted to invest seriously in PR. You'll recall that our start-up budget for the company was $15,000, so when we were looking at a five-figure investment to work with a New York–based PR company, it was a huge deal for us. But we wanted to take Admiral Road to the next level and thought that retaining PR professionals was the best way to do it. We dipped heavily into our bank account and put all our eggs into one basket. We decided that if we lost that money, it wouldn't kill us. We wouldn't love it, to be sure, but it wouldn't sink us either.

A hotshot young account exec was assigned to work on our project. She was green, keen, and she was great. She pitched our story to newspapers, magazines, and TV shows. And on the day that one of Amy's kids was born, she called the hospital to tell us that she got our blanket into *InStyle* magazine—and not just any issue, but the holiday issue. We were going to be in the Christmas Gift Guide—the Holy Grail of the magazine world. We were getting our Big Break.

We did a market-sizing exercise. We determined that even if a small percentage of the millions of *InStyle* readers bought our blankets, it would change our company. We were beside ourselves anticipating the orders that would come in. We were terrified that we wouldn't be able to meet demand.

The magazine hit the stands and Gwyneth Paltrow was on the freakin' cover! We had won the lottery!

Then three things happened—and none of them was good. First, the magazine came out late—around the end of November. Since our blankets are made-to-order, we can't just pop a product in a box when we receive an order. There is a turnaround time required for production. It was very late in the season for people to be purchasing customized gifts to be delivered in time for Christmas. We were counting on the issue coming out a week or two earlier. Most people had probably already finished their Christmas shopping by the time the magazine was released.

Second, the magazine neglected to include our website address. Sure, our toll-free number was listed, but you kind of want your customers to be able to find you online. Since the photo of the blanket wasn't huge (think postage stamp), not having our website mentioned was far from ideal. So between the late publication date and the lack of website information, our sales from the magazine were lower than we'd expected. Much lower.

But wait—there's still more. We had a shipping disaster. It was one of our busiest pre-Christmas shipping days and we sent dozens of "*InStyle*" orders to the United States. The shipment got lost. The whole darn thing. Fell off a truck at the border never to be seen again. It was a complete nightmare. We were remaking and reshipping orders right up until Christmas—and some after Christmas too, all at our expense. This was not a happy confluence of events.

We took a gamble. We put a real dent in our corporate piggy bank. We built the idea, and they did not come. We did everything right and thought that we had hit it big. And then it didn't materialize.

All of this was going on during the Christmas season—far and away our busiest time of year. We were exhibiting at a major show and were already fragile from exhaustion. When a friend of Danielle's popped by the show and asked her why we hadn't thought to provide *InStyle* magazine with our web address (obviously we had), Danielle just cracked. The tears sprang. Why? Because she had the realization that after all our hard work, our business wouldn't be dramatically different. We had invested all that time and money, and we weren't going to be propelled to the next level. We thought that we were holding the winning lottery ticket, and then we learned that a few of the numbers were actually a little bit off. Seeing her old friend who worked at a fancy downtown job, shopping on her lunch hour, just threw Danielle over the edge.

When the dust settled, we had a chance to evaluate what had happened. It was true, we hadn't received the thousands of orders that we thought we might. But we were still standing. The results of all the exposure that the PR firm garnered *had* helped grow our business—it just didn't "supersize" us the way we had hoped. We had to accept the fact that we were simply going to have to keep slogging away. And it was a bitter pill to swallow.

In fact, once we hired the PR firm, we even abandoned our

regular business planning efforts. With PR we imagined that we'd get a ton of exposure, we'd have zillions of new customers, and then we wouldn't have to work to grow our business. Ever again. Why would we plan?

Clearly, when Oprah didn't come calling, we had to refocus and hit the drawing board again. We spent the next year planning and implementing all the projects that we had ever dreamed of since starting Admiral Road. We learned that publicity is simply one way to achieve growth. We realized that if we were going to stick with it, it was going to be a slog.

The big slog

The slog is not something that we have faced alone. We met one savvy mompreneur who runs a high-end corporate gift company. She was exasperated when telling us, "I just can't believe it's such a slog." This, from a woman who turned her back on an incredibly successful corporate career to run her own company! It's extremely tough to realize that your accomplishments in the corporate world don't always translate into quick self-employed success.

Elisa Palter and her partner sold their small business after sixteen years. This is what Elisa says about the uphill climb that has been their journey:

"Our growth was a gradual process. We just kept plugging away. Each year we'd look up and say, 'We'll give it one more year.' We always questioned whether what we were taking out was worth all the effort we were putting in. We never had that 'Oprah moment' where things just took off. The first five years were a real slog. We each took turns feeling up when the other was down. Now, for the hours we work, we couldn't make much more working for someone else."

Unless your rise is meteoric, you will have to toil away at your business to ensure that it is continuing to thrive—much in the same way you do with your children.

22

Duking it out

Competition and making the best of business rivalry

We wish that we could tell you that all of your experiences with competition will be good ones. We'd like to be able to tell you that there exists a sisterhood of mompreneurs who treat each other as they would like to be treated. We want to tell you that you won't be blatantly ripped off by another mompreneur if you so much as hint at success. We guess it's possible that this will be your reality, but you'd certainly be unusual.

Here's the real deal. Dealing with competition will most likely be a big part of your mompreneur experience. While it can eat up a lot of your time and energy, it's not all bad by any means. There are pluses and minuses to going head-to-head with other companies.

First, the bad news.

Competition can take up a lot of your time and energy

Remember how we talked about the importance of setting a plan and following it, rather than reacting to every little thing that comes up? Well, a business rivalry can easily have you reacting left, right, and centre. It goes something like this: The competition has a sale . . . wait—should I have a sale? The competition is offering a new product or service . . . all of a sudden you're thinking about whether you should be in that market too.

We've got one mompreneur friend who has dedicated so much energy to her competitors that it almost hurts to watch. Every time the other company does anything, she feels that she has to do it too, only better. The sad thing is that hers is the superior company in every way, and we wish she'd just stop worrying about what the other gal is doing.

Robyn Green-Ruskin of Movies for Mommies has gone head to head with some much larger companies but still has a great attitude about competing. She says, "I know how my offering is distinctive. It's counterproductive to stress. You just have to focus inwardly and be positive. Negativity doesn't get you anywhere."

And Nicole Garza of Mally Designs says, "Competition will happen. I can't stop it. But I have a choice about how to handle it. One of my competitors lives in the same small town. I decided to remain pleasant and focus on making our product the best that it can be."

Just as you can determine how much attention you'll give to your kids when they misbehave, you can also choose not to be irked by annoying competitors.

Competition can be expensive

So what do you do when you're being unfairly treated by a competitor? Unfortunately, it often involves paying a lawyer exorbitant amounts of money to make it stop. In our experience, it depends on the severity of the situation, and we've certainly had to bring the lawyers in, but we've also found that a well-crafted email or letter can often make someone smarten up.

We know mompreneurs who paid lawyers to write letters and

were unsuccessful, and ladies who sued the pants off another mom. Not only is it a huge distraction from your business, it's a crappy use of your money. Our advice is to protect yourself up front. Here's what Julie Kenney of Jewels and Pinstripes says: "Having agreements and going through the trademark process has protected me—I feel fortunate that I was so smart. Sometimes you have to let it roll off your back. But I'll fight to every last dollar to protect my brand and my customers."

Candace Alper of Name Your Tunes advises, "Know what you need to do to protect yourself legally and structurally. It's expensive but it could save you a lot in the end." Trademark, patent, get contracts, sign agreements, etc. You'll still be paying the lawyers, but at least it's on your terms and in your own best interest.

Competition can be nasty and personal

You might be surprised to find out that there is a fair bit of sketchy imitation going on even within the mompreneur community. Despite our backgrounds in big business, we were pretty shocked to see how some mompreneurs can treat each other. We weren't prepared for some of the behaviour among the sisterhood.

Here's what Candace Alper has to say: "Competition is good. There is room in the market. The problem comes when the competition is a personal betrayal or if the competitor is personally nasty and doesn't play fair. When an employee or customer steals from you it's hard to treat it as a business issue—it becomes personal. This is especially hard when it comes from other mompreneurs. As moms we all have the same goals. We want to teach our kids right from wrong—to be moral people. Then, when a mom turns around and steals from you, it can be hard to understand."

Jennifer Torres of Salsa Babies echoes this sentiment: "I've had my name, logo, and web content stolen. Someone has recreated the graphic we have of *me* depicted with my baby! I'm not afraid of competition. What annoys me is when people steal my work and use it—especially other moms. I've had ongoing legal battles. But the worst is that it can really bother me. I get angry and upset. I constantly battle with how much I want to focus on dealing with these people and how much I want to just focus on my own business."

As for us, we've had our fair share of questionable imitation from within the mompreneur community. Once a woman from the other side of the country emailed us with some *very* specific questions about our business—the kind of thing that no one would ever provide to anyone else, least of all someone who happened to also make personalized baby blankets. Since we were intrigued to see who could be asking us these questions, we looked at her website, only to find that she had copied the "About Us" section of our website. She had changed a few words here and there but had otherwise just copied it verbatim. We sent her a stern email letting her know that the area of the website was supposed to be "About Her" and she quickly changed her site.

In more than one instance, we've had competitors contact our suppliers and resellers posing as someone other than who they were to try to find out about our business model. And our biggest competitor once stole an entire section of our website—in fact, they had forgotten to remove the words "Admiral Road" from it. Apparently, if a customer had a problem with one of the other company's blankets, they were meant to contact us!

But here's our favourite competition story. One day an acquaintance ordered blankets to be sent home to his niece and nephew in his native Hungary. We heard from him after they were delivered and he let us know how thrilled everyone was with the blankets. About a year later, Amy bumped into him and he told her that a relative of his in Hungary had been so impressed with our blankets that they decided to open a personalized blanket company selling blankets that looked a whole lot like ours. He told us this in the spirit of flattery, so that's how we decided to take it. After all, our share in the Hungarian personalized blanket market has always been—um—slim. Besides, from time to time, we do wonder how things are going over there at Hungarian Admiral Road.

Closer to home, we've had designs plain ripped off—as well as our branding, language, new products, and more. It sounds amusing now, but the truth is that it caused us a lot of angst at the time. After all, we'd invested the time, money, and sweat in each aspect of our business and we loathed that others were taking shortcuts at our expense.

Nearly all of the mompreneurs we spoke to have had negative experiences with mompreneur competitors. It makes you wonder just what is going on. Here's our theory: we think there is a quiet desperation on the part of mothers to find an alternative to returning to work outside the home. The idea of leaving the kids all day and going back to a family-unfriendly environment is so unpalatable that they feel they must embark upon their own business. They have to find a way to make it work. The desperation, we think, can lead to taking shortcuts with their businesses. That being said, we're going on record saying there is no excuse, ever, for stealing another mompreneur's work.

We're not knocking fair and square competition. Every single mompreneur we spoke to said they were perfectly happy to compete fairly. In fact, there are some real benefits of competition. Let's take a look.

Competition helps to raise awareness about what you do

The reality is that consumers aren't all that loyal to one particular company, no matter how good the brand and how dependable the customer service. They may want to start with the company they first heard of, but more than anything people are busy and just need to get the job done. If one of your competitors is attending trade shows, advertising, and generally educating the public about the need for the good or service you provide, you're naturally going to benefit from that. Sara Bingham, founder of WeeHands, benefited tremendously from the marketing initiatives of a competitor when she was starting up. The competitor attended baby shows and created a demand for baby sign language classes, but it seemed the parents weren't overly concerned about who provided the service. Sara took advantage of this, started up in the wake of this newly created demand, and hasn't looked back. She continues to be pleased to be confused with the competition.

Sarah Morgenstern and Minnow Hamilton of SavvyMom.ca also benefited from competitors launching around the same time as them. They say, "Competition kept us going. We wanted to be the first to market, but a number of other players launched at the same time. It was a good thing for us. We always knew we were going to be the best of the companies out there, but competition made us be. It helped us keep the drive alive. Also, one of our competitors ended up paving the way for us in terms of establishing the business model with customers."

Your competitors are smart

Just like you've got great ideas and have developed some great practices, so too has the competition. And just like they're watching you, you should be watching them. But know that there's a distinction between being inspired by the best practices of others in your sector and ripping them off.

Victoria Sopik of Kids & Company always looks to see what the competition is doing, despite the fact that she is by far the largest player in her space. Victoria says, "I always think people should look at the competition. Even though we are head and shoulders above our competition, I still spend time looking at what other daycare centres are doing. We've tried some of the things we've learned from competitors' websites and have been thrilled with the results." They've learned from the best practices of other companies and have adapted some of them to Kids & Company.

Mompreneur Jordan Maher learned a lot from watching a rival company that came to market around the same time and outlasted her first venture. She tells us, "My competition really made me want to up my game—they taught me what I needed to do."

You can also look to your competitors to gain broader market knowledge. Anne-Sophie Falconer of Lumiere Kids keeps abreast of her competitors to see what types of items reappear on the shelves season after season, and what the general market and design trends are.

Your competitors understand your reality

A former business school classmate said something a while back which is probably one of the kindest things anyone has ever said to us. She said, "I can see how people would underestimate the complexities of a business like yours." The truth is, no one else ever really appreciates the challenges of running your business—except someone who is running a very similar one.

As long as everyone is playing fairly, there can be a great opportunity to get along with other players in your sector, and to trade war stories, if nothing else. Lolita Carrico, single mom of two boys and founder of MyGloss.com, was the creator of the very successful web community ModernMom.com. Lolita found competition to be a blessing: "I found there was room in the market for both me and my competitor, and working together provided benefits for all of us. Some of my closest friends are my competitors."

We've been cordial with our competitors as long as everyone was being respectful, but we've found our closest mompreneur friends among those who compete in a similar, but not identical, category.

Andrea Page of FitMom has taken a more open approach: "I've tried hard to have good relationships with my competitors—I think there are ways we can work together. I think that's a more female approach." You'll recall that as newcomer Jennifer Torres of Salsa Babies came onto the scene, Andrea chose to embrace and help her rather than be intimidated by her. Today the two are good friends.

Your competitors will motivate you

Ask anyone who's had a close encounter with the competition and they'll likely tell you that they accelerated their efforts immediately after. Tricia Mumby of Mabel's Labels says competition is "ugly but it's also been the best thing for us. It set us on fire and has probably been the number one motivator in our business. We need something scary to really get us going." And Julie Kenney of Jewels and Pinstripes tells us, "Competition makes me stronger and more fierce and innovative."

In the personalized blanket category, we had a year where a healthy handful of competitors jumped onto the scene all at once. Some of them did some pretty annoying things, like ripping off our designs and marketing materials. It did succeed in making us sufficiently motivated to focus and drive harder. We did more in the year that followed than we ever have in our business. When we got frustrated, we just kept repeating to ourselves *"Smarter, better, faster."*

The fact of the matter is that you can get pretty complacent about your business until someone threatens it. Then, when it is threatened, you can kick it into gear in a whole new way. Rivalry can make you leaner, more efficient, and a heck of a lot more creative. Odds are it'll probably relight the fire you had when you first thought of your business. Just like you wouldn't want anything to threaten your own child, you're not going to let your business come to any harm either. Competition can make your business much, much better. In fact, we hope you have a bit of it—but not too much.

Competition helps you figure out who you are

There's nothing like seeing your competition wade into new waters to make you think about what works best for you. We've seen competitors take very different routes, and with each step we've been able to evaluate their offering versus our own. It has helped us enormously to define who we are—often by determining who we are not.

Sara Bingham of WeeHands has had a similar experience: "Competition has made me clarify what WeeHands is: an original program, well-trained instructors, and the most developed curriculum. It drives you forward. In fact, WeeHands wouldn't be where it is without competition."

So you see, there are some great things about putting it all out there and letting the best woman win. It's all in the way you look at it.

So now you've got the skinny on competition in the world of mompreneurship. It's a reality, but how you handle it is up to you. Of course there are going to be factors beyond your control, but ultimately the choice is yours. You can get bogged down in it or you can embrace the battle and all of the positive effects of competition. However it works out for you, we wish you good luck and remind you that karma's a bitch—but it's got nothing on a mompreneur scorned.

23

Grow, baby, grow

Taking your business to the next level

So you've taken some time to think about how your business is doing. No matter how good business is, we'll bet you'd like it to be better. This raises the question, what can you do to continue to grow?

RECOMMENDED READING: *THE E-MYTH*

"E-Myth" (or Entrepreneurial Myth) refers to an idea articulated in a book by the same name by Michael Gerber. Gerber argues that there is a high rate of small-business failure because people are inspired to start businesses, but then don't have adequate knowledge of how to run the business. (Pick up a copy of the book—you'll be glad you did.)

—Prof. Reuber

Now that you're ticking along, a question has probably crept from the back of your mind to the front: What next? It's time to think about how big your business can become (or how big you want it to be) and how to get there smartly. When we hit this phase at Admiral Road, Becky gave us some great advice that we still come back to time and time again: Narrow your focus and broaden your market. How can you do what you do even better, and reach more people?

In order to really grow, you need to think about how you're going to do it. In this chapter, we'll have a look at how to make the most of your business by evaluating your offering, exploring new channels and products, and looking at where to get money to fund your business growth. Onward!

Your offering—does it still make sense?

Before you think about how to grow your business further, it may pay to step back and make sure you're in the right business to begin with.

As we've mentioned, in the early days of your business a little flexibility can go a long way. We've been asked repeatedly why we named ourselves Admiral Road and not something like "Fuzzy Baby Blanket Company." The truth is that we didn't know who we were going to be when we grew up in terms of our product line, and we didn't want to limit ourselves with our name. We wanted to have some time to experiment with different products and product mixes.

Believe it or not, naming ourselves Admiral Road wasn't a random decision. We even consulted an advertising guru. We started the business in the basement of Amy's dad's house at a time when he really needed company. We spent many hours toiling away down there, as well as many hours sitting on his couch upstairs, helping him get through a difficult time. The house on Admiral Road held a lot of meaning for us. Admiral Road is also a charming street in an old, downtown-Toronto neighbourhood. Those in the city who know of the street have a lovely impression of it. Finally, "Admiral" starts with the letter "A." Whenever we attend trade shows, we're at the top of the list, and we've always found that a good place to be.

Within the first two years, it became clear that we were a mail-order personalized baby blanket company. We're glad we have a clear sense of who we are today—it guides us constantly and helps us make decisions more easily. But we couldn't have come up with that sense of corporate identity had we not played with our mix in the early days.

Now that you've been a mompreneur for a few years, it's time to evaluate whether your offering still makes sense. Are you still enjoying what you're doing? Is there a market for your business? Are your customers demanding new or different things from you? This is the time to scale back on certain initiatives, start new ones, or stay the course and keep plowing forward.

FAMOUS WORDS

Insanity: doing the same thing over and over again and expecting different results.

—Albert Einstein

At this point, if you're doing things in your business that aren't working, stop immediately! You've been at it long enough that it won't get better. Maybe it's a certain product that just never flew (even though you love it). Maybe it's a service that your customers just aren't that interested in (even though you love the idea). Maybe it's a trade show where you've never made your money back.

Some mompreneurs told us that they didn't evaluate their offering early enough to make the changes necessary. While Quita Alfred genuinely wanted her vision for her quilt business to work out, she says, "I kept offering the product that I loved but I didn't do a good job of giving the customers what they wanted." By continually evaluating your offering you can be flexible and stay on the road to growth.

We've talked about Nicole Morell, who owns Honey-bunch. com. Prior to running her children's toy and gift shop online only, Nicole also ran a brick-and-mortar shop for several years. With the hours that retail requires, the location of her store, and the demands of her young children, she learned that she "needed to change the formula." Seeing the potential in the Internet, Nicole now wants to become "the destination website for children's products in Canada." There's nothing wrong with changing direction. It's smart, in fact, to realize where the market is headed and where you want to go with your business.

There's a time in a young woman's life when taking off with a backpack to find herself is perfectly acceptable. We're guessing that, in business, you won't have the luxury of time or travel to find yourself—but whatever it takes, it's worth the effort to be clear on your offering. Once you're perfectly clear about who you are and what you do, you can begin to tackle new initiatives for growth.

Exploring new markets

Exploring new markets means doing exactly what you're doing, but doing it in new places or for a new group of people. You sell the same product or service using the same channels—you just have to find ways to sell more of it.

Entering new markets may mean working harder and spending more money. At Admiral Road, we've tested new markets by attending trade shows in different cities. We've literally taken the show on the road to "seed" our product in new markets.

But putting your company into new markets doesn't have to be costly. Pitching yourself to a different audience can be done cost effectively. For example, while we typically sell our blankets as new baby gifts, we have also targeted the summer camp market and offered blankets to take to camp. You don't have to change your product much or the way you sell it, you just need to sell it to new and different people.

Exploring new channels

A channel refers to where you sell product. Exploring new channels means taking what you already offer and looking at new ways and places to sell it. For example, if you already wholesale your product, maybe you'll create a retail website. Or a personal trainer who has worked with clients one-on-one might think about offering specialized group classes.

Mompreneur Martha Scully thinks about growth in terms of staying true to her offering. She says, "I'm always thinking of ways to expand—geographically and with our current and past customers. Another mompreneur once told me, 'Only stick with what you know—don't venture off into other things.' So, I try to expand my existing business."

Sometimes an experiment doesn't go as planned. You think you're on the right track, but the numbers just don't back it up. Mompreneur Alison Lim of Style Kid ran a successful online business before deciding to open a retail store. This is what Alison says of the experience: "A retail store was never my dream, but one of my long-term employees was very keen on it and it seemed like a good idea. It became apparent that retail and online are very different businesses that have different needs. There wasn't much cohesion between the businesses—the customers and the products tended to be different and it really required separate management. I closed the store a year later—it was a very easy decision."

It's okay to try new things. Just make sure you pull the plug before your experiment goes all Frankenstein on you.

Mompreneur Sara Bingham of WeeHands is creating a line of educational CDs and DVDs. She's delivering the same sign language product as her classes offer, she's just using different channels to reach her customers.

WeeHands, Salsa Babies, Movies for Mommies, and SupperWorks are all businesses that started as one-off ventures. None of these mompreneurs anticipated expanding their businesses and delivering their offerings in this way. Through licensing and franchising, they're able to reach wider audiences than they ever expected.

Exploring new channels: Our story

Not too long ago, we had an experience with trying a new channel. The results were illuminating, if not overly profitable. We decided that we would try to enter the world of children's apparel and become a manufacturer and wholesaler of a collection of fun and functional items for kids. With all of our children accounted for (the last was en route), we were ready for a new challenge in our business.

We had an idea for a really cute and innovative kid's scarf. We'd tested this new product at a big craft show to great success and we were sure that we were on to something.

Armed with the knowledge that we had a great product, we decided to plan our entree into the children's apparel market. Unlike our beginnings with Admiral Road, we knew that we'd be dealing with a whole new customer—retail store buyers. So we needed to appear professional, slick, and ready to play with the big guys.

In order to be competitive on price, we decided to manufacture overseas. In short, the process was complicated, time-consuming, and didn't mesh with our corporate identity. (Our model of home sewers who knew and loved our children was a long way from mass production in China.)

We undertook a media blitz that couldn't have gone better. Our scarves were featured in national magazines, trade publications, and newspapers. And then we debuted our scarves at some high-profile children's apparel shows. While the scarves were quite well received, it was nowhere near the same reaction we'd received at our craft shows. This was a different audience altogether.

We also learned. Boy, did we learn. We talked to every single person who would speak to us. We asked questions. And more questions. At our first big children's wear show, we were lucky enough to meet experienced vendors who were willing to share their knowledge. One of our neighbours at the show had an established line and was selling in six hundred stores and bringing in nearly $1 million in revenue. We were impressed—until he told us that he wasn't actually making any money. (You'll recall what we said about the difference between bringing in revenue and actually making a living.) We also watched this guy nearly drowning in the stress of managing his sizeable company. He was frantically on his cellphone and laptop all week. It wasn't the most appealing example.

We also learned that our customers would mostly be small-shop owners. This was a customer we were unfamiliar with. With Admiral Road, we really understood our customers and how to communicate with them. But we were unsure about this new group. The store owners were running small businesses too—and scrambling to manage cash flow. They'd place orders and then ask us to call for payment when we were ready to ship. Only we learned that it was hard—really hard—to get that payment. We realized that we weren't set up for the kind of selling and account management required for a wholesale operation. More importantly, we realized that we didn't like it. Spending time chasing money (never a part of the Admiral Road business model) does not rank high on our list of things that we enjoy.

So, there we were, about one year into our new venture. Remember how we said one year in is a good time to take stock? We knew that there were two paths ahead of us. The first was to go even harder. We had mittens and hat prototypes ready to roll out, with more ideas in the pipeline. We'd bring in sales reps and develop our sales (and harassment!) skills. It would all cost a lot more money—but there was potential to really grow.

The second option was to get out before we spent any more money on a venture that wasn't really up our alley. And that's what we chose to do. We thought about what it had taken to bring Admiral Road up to be a nice little company, and then we thought about running Admiral Road, raising five kids, and scaling another new business mountain. Quite honestly, we didn't have the time or energy to pour into a large-scale new venture just then.

We still sell the apparel products—but we manufacture locally and sell within our own retail distribution channels. We love the creative element and our customers love the products. Ultimately, we've broken even on the wholesale apparel project and still have our lovely brand and trade show booth with us for the day we want to do something with it. The brand and the products are great—but it's not the business for us right now.

The funny thing is that we don't consider this a failure in any sense. It was an experiment with a new direction—and what we learned was invaluable. From it, we understood what we love about our first baby, Admiral Road, and the directions that are more appealing to us. Our new projects are about a thousand times more rewarding than calling Maggie at her store in Wichita and asking, again, for her credit card information.

At the end of the day, we're glad we ventured into this new market. It helped us define who we are and where we're going. We hope your misadventures are equally as fruitful!

Exploring new products

If it doesn't make sense to explore new channels, another way to grow your business is to expand your product line. Once you've got your first product up and running, you might think about how to get more "wallet share" from your customers. If they love coming to you for a certain product, maybe they'll spend even more money with you if you can offer them more of what they want.

What other products can you offer your customers that build on your existing business?

Eryn Green and Tamar Wagman of Sweetpea Baby Food and Organic Snacks have leveraged their frozen organic baby food business to launch a line of organic cookies aimed at toddlers. Entering the market with products for older babies allows them to hang on to their customers longer. Remember how we told you about Victoria Sopik's childcare company? Well, she has found ways to keep families with her longer by offering school-age programs, back-up childcare for families with alternative childcare arrangements, and even eldercare to help working families with the challenge of caring for aging parents. We talked about the cost of acquiring a customer. So, getting more revenue from the same customer sounds pretty good, doesn't it?

Where do you get the cash for all this growth?

It's true—you need to spend money to make money. With this universal truth in your back pocket, you'll need to consider where the money is going to come from. You can beg. You can borrow. We wouldn't recommend stealing. So here are some ways you can think about your financial options.

Inject more of your money

Many small businesses self-finance to start out. You scrape together what's in your chequing account, or you cash in your RRSPs, or your family gives you money to help you get started. But what do you do when you're already down the path and you still need money? It's completely personal how much money you're comfortable contributing to your business. There are no guarantees in business. One question you can ask yourself to help determine your answer is "How would I feel if I lost this money?" If you're considering investing more of your own money, make sure that you and your life partner are on the same page.

If your business is profitable, you can reinvest the profits back into the business to finance further growth. One of the mompreneurs behind the SupperWorks franchise tells us, "We have achieved our goals but we're still in growth mode and have sunk everything back into the company."

This is something we did at Admiral Road for years. It was our preference to delay personal gratification rather than pay someone else to borrow money. Now, there were a few years in there that we truly did not enjoy working for free. It's just that we would have enjoyed taking out the money for ourselves, only to borrow it from somewhere else, even less.

Borrow

From our experience, this is a popular choice. You can look to a bank loan, take out a line of credit, or borrow money from your family. In our early years, we experienced a cash crunch in the middle of the year. We were at the height of production and spending, but hadn't yet hit our late-year revenue boon. We went to our banker to get a short-term line of credit to bridge the gap.

Carol Pitre runs Kid Brother Clothing, a retail clothing line for boys. Last year she decided to pursue a wholesale strategy and knew she couldn't finance her start-up effort with her existing cash flow. She was four years into her business when she went to the bank for her first loan to finance her growth plans. She says, "I know that never assuming debt in the past has inhibited my growth."

Seek investors

One way to take your company to the next level is to seek investors. You'll get access to their chequebooks and hopefully their business expertise, and in exchange you'll have to give away part of your company.

We know mompreneur companies that have taken on investors in the hope of growing their businesses dramatically. Investors bring the cash, but there are going to be strings attached. Investors will want a chunk of your company, and a say in how things are run.

BE A SOCIAL BUTTERFLY: HOW TO FIND INVESTORS TO FINANCE GROWTH

It's difficult to get investors interested in your business. Their interest will be heightened if you can show that:

- You have committed customers now and a plan for acquiring new ones.
- You have an advantage in the market that can be protected from competitors (e.g., a patent, valuable R&D know-how, a brand, a large engaged online community, a hard-to-replicate location).
- Your business is on track to becoming cash-flow positive.

As well, potential investors will want to know that their money is safe in your hands and they can work with you. They will want to know that you are realistic about ceding some control and ownership to them, and that you are willing to learn from them.

Investors are hard to find. Some communities have organizations of "angels"—private individuals who are interested in investing in businesses. They generally invest between $20,000 and $250,000 in businesses located close to where they live and in industries in which they have some experience.

In looking for investors, leverage your social ties. People are more apt to invest in the businesses of people they know because they have a better idea of their talents, and there would be social sanctions from dishonest behaviour. Likewise, investors value indirect social ties, or referrals from someone they know. The reason for this is that most people are reluctant to recommend someone whom they think may fail to a friend or business contact. So, if you think you will be looking for investment capital, developing your network should be a priority.

—Prof. Reuber

So now you've got the tools to think about growing your business: exploring new markets, new channels, and new product opportunities, not to mention financing new growth. Next stop: world domination. But first, let's take a moment to think about how you'll manage all that growth.

24

Putting your house in order

How to get organized for growth

If you're a few years in and growing like gangbusters, you'll find that your little company ain't what it used to be. As we've raised our kids, we've learned that parenting doesn't get easier as the kids grow, just different. The same can be said of your business. You may need to make some changes along the way to be poised to deal with this growth. We've found that taking the time to sort yourself out—whether by getting organized, hiring help, or finding extra available cash—can save you a lot in the end.

In this chapter, we want to make sure that you're running your business as efficiently as possible. This is the time to evaluate how your business operates and where there is room for improvement. You'll want to consider how you spend your time and which parts of your business can be standardized or outsourced.

Thinking outside the box

On your journey towards efficiency, ask yourself if you're in a rut in any part of your business. Here's a story about how we unstuck ourselves from our processes.

When we bought our business from its owner, Betty, she told us how to get things done. She showed us how to neatly pack up a blanket for shipping and gave us the name of her box supplier.

So when we set up shop, we contacted the box supplier and set up an account of our own. We placed an order for the exact same boxes. (We can't tell you how fun it was to unload one thousand of those boxes off a semi parked in the middle of a residential street with Amy eight months pregnant. In November.) For years, we shipped out blankets in these boxes.

As a mail-order company, one issue that has always plagued us is the high cost of shipping. One day we did an analysis on our shipping expenses and it occurred to us that we could save on shipping costs if we changed how we packed our blankets and reduced the size of our box. As it turned out, not only were smaller boxes significantly cheaper, but we reduced our shipping expense by about twenty percent. And we could warehouse our new smaller boxes more easily.

It seemed we had been, well, stuck in the box. Once upon a time, someone told us to do something a certain way, so out of trust and laziness, we did. Sure, those old boxes worked just fine, but clearly there was a better solution out there waiting for us.

We use this example to demonstrate that we all get stuck in ruts. Now that you're a few years into your business, it's time to pull up your socks and take a good look around. In all likelihood, there are inefficiencies in your business that are costing you time and money.

One mompreneur we know owns a retail business. She says, "Sometimes I think I'm in a rut. I think that I could be doing more for the store by being out of store—networking, being more connected to what's going on around me." Indeed, sometimes the way to figure out how to do better at what you're doing is to talk to other people. Whether it's your husband, a business coach, or a networking group, you should consider bringing in others to help "audit" your business. If you need to, you can also do this on your own. Just start by listing all the main categories in your business and thinking through how you execute each component: prime suspects are sales and marketing, finances, and accounting and operations.

Rarely—only very rarely—do we bring in the husbands to discuss Admiral Road. In fact, we've only formally summoned their opinions once in eight years. But one time, a few years into our business, we held a four-person summit. We were poised for growth and we knew it. We just didn't know exactly how to get there. During that summit, one of our husbands said, "I think your business is great and I don't have much to say about it. I think you could grow this into a really big company. I only want to say that you need to spend your time on revenue-generating activities. You need to focus on marketing. You cannot keep packing up boxes. That's it."

Right after that summit, we hired our first in-house employee—to pack boxes. Of course we knew that we needed to take this next step. We just needed a little push from someone outside our company—even if it was a husband—to start thinking outside the box.

Setting standards

Years ago we met a mompreneur who now runs a multi-million-dollar company. A huge turning point for her, she says, was when the company standardized its approach to customer service. No longer did they have to deal with customer-related issues on the fly. In our experience, it takes a lot of energy and effort to deal with customer service issues on a one-off basis. Inspired by this mompreneur, we put customer service standards in place ourselves. That means if a certain situation arises, we have a specific way of dealing with it. We know how to handle the issue and our staff does too. Standards have simply taken time and tension out of the equation.

We've also tried to be more efficient in our roles. This doesn't mean that we don't talk about our roles within the context of our partnership, or even that we can't switch our job responsibilities around. But now, for example, one of us oversees blanket production and one of us oversees orders and customer service. In the beginning, we both wanted to learn and understand all aspects of the business. But now, being clear-cut in our roles has only helped our efficiency.

Ordering your supplies and inventory is another way you can probably stand to be more efficient. They say that past actions are the best indicators of future performance. If you've been keeping track of your sales (and, pretty please, we hope you have been!), all the data you need to make decisions about ordering and supplies and inventory are at your fingertips. So use it. Look at your past sales records to help you gauge what sales should look like down the road.

There is a phrase from our stints in management consulting that has stayed with us: "getting stuck in the weeds." Back then it referred to getting bogged down in a strategic issue, being overwhelmed, or struggling. It's so easy to get stuck in the weeds of your business. There are so many things—like customer service issues and dealing with your suppliers—that can wear you down if you don't have an effective way to deal with them. The toddler years of your business are a great opportunity to get strategic and straighten things out. You've seen those kids at the park who have never been disciplined, right? Well, we recommend that you take control of your business now. It's not too late.

Cleaning up the shop

Once a year, when spring comes, we're all supposed to clean our houses from top to bottom—or so they say! Well, if you've been working on your business for a while, it's probably due for some spring cleaning too. No doubt there are some issues in your business that have been shoved aside in favour of more urgent matters.

As hard as it is to carve out the time to clean house, it will be well worth your effort. It's a bit like going to the gym or having sex— you may not always want to ahead of time, but you're always glad that you did.

FIVE TIPS FOR BUSINESS SPRING CLEANING

1. Check in with your suppliers to see if you can negotiate better rates.
2. Get up-to-date with your email correspondence by cleaning out your inbox.
3. File your paperwork and archive your old files.
4. Meet with your accountant to make sure that your books are in order. Then get ahead of your tax filing.
5. Pay a teenager to help you clean up your junk. Give away what you can and chuck what you can't. You won't believe what a preschool is happy to take off your hands.

When you can find a spare moment, take the time to clean house. We assure you that it will be worth it.

ARE YOU READY TO LEAVE HOME?

Some mompreneurs love working from home and some find it a giant headache. And then there are those who are literally driven out of the house by their business. Here's what a few of the mompreneurs had to say.

Love it

I've actually come full circle and am home again. I gave up teaching the baby signing classes, which was hard to let go of, because it allows me to be home and available to my kids, which was my main goal. If I'm at work in the basement I can drop what I'm doing if the school calls.

—Sara Bingham, WeeHands

In limbo

My goal is to either buy a bigger house so I have more space for my business or maybe rent office space. I think that would help me to work during work hours only and avoid working evenings and weekends.

—Anita MacCallum, bookkeeper

Leave it

When we were in my home it was constant chaos. We moved out of my house after two years. With the office, we get more done while we're at work. It also helps to manage the expectations of my kids and husband—when I'm at the office I can focus on business and not be interrupted by family issues that might not necessarily require my attention. When I'm home, I can spend more time with my family without feeling the pull of the office in the next room. The separation allows me to focus on one thing at a time.

—Minnow Hamilton, SavvyMom.ca

Outsource

Anne-Sophie Falconer of Lumiere Kids is a creative talent. She channels her energy into making beautiful things for children and loves when people appreciate the work that she does. She also loves the flexibility of being available for her two daughters. But the worst thing, she says, about running her own business is "the stuff I don't like to do—like marketing and accounting." We think lots of business people can relate to the difficulty in getting the hard stuff done.

Now that you're out of the newborn phase, it's time to pull up and have a look around. What are you working on in your business? At this point, it's time to work on what you're good at and outsource or hire for the rest where it makes sense.

If your sales have grown, you've probably needed help to accomplish that. It might be time to ask yourself a question that we once had to ask ourselves: Is everyone getting paid but you? One mompreneur told us about a time when one of her employees got snippy with her. "Hey!" she wanted to yell. "You're making more money than I am!" Of course she said nothing, but we've heard versions of that story over and over again. And believe us, we're no strangers to the feeling that we're at the end of the money line.

OUTSOURCE SMARTLY

It makes sense to outsource as long as the skill isn't key to your success or is in short supply, so your business doesn't become dependent on an outside party you have little control over.

—Prof. Reuber

We think you're more likely to stick with your business if you're enjoying it. Outsourcing the tasks that you find mundane or just don't have the ability to do well will help to keep your business fresh for you. It will also help you focus on the revenue-generating projects that will propel your growth. The only trick with outsourcing is managing your costs. If you need to outsource, make sure that your pricing structure still makes sense. And consider tweaking your pricing if you need to.

FROM THE MOUTHS OF MOMS

Trish Magwood ran her own company for ten years. When describing herself, she says, "I'm incredibly focused. I thrive in the new, and the unstructured. I love to come up with ideas, but I don't love the execution, the nitty-gritty. I like to be busy and I thrive on the chaos." We think she's onto something when she says, "I think you should be aware of what you like—it's probably what you're good at."

Hiring—how to bring other people into your company

Lots of mompreneur businesses start off as one-woman shows. If you grow, you'll need to bring people into your company to help you execute your offering.

After working so hard and so long to bring your vision to life, taking on other people in your little company can be a strange thing. It was for us. You've worked alone, developed your own processes and systems, and then one day someone walks through your door and everything changes—hopefully for the better.

Hiring can be an adjustment, for sure. You've figured out your own quirky ways of doing things, and now you need to share your dirty little secrets with someone else. But your staff just may save you from yourself and help you get back some of the balance you strove for in the first place. Let's chat about the benefits and challenges involved in hiring, according to the mompreneurs.

Benefits

Hiring allows you to focus on what you're good at

If you can work on what you enjoy and what you're good at, you have a better shot at sticking with your business and being successful. One mompreneur says, "I'm really good at operations, but for many years I couldn't focus on that because I was the sales girl, the client services girl, the invoice girl. Now that we have a team, I can focus on leading the company, and the way that I lead it is through the operations. That's the most key thing in the company. The key to success in life is focusing on what you're good at."

Building a support team will allow you to continue working to achieve your goal in the best way you know how.

HELP ON THE MOM FRONT

Although we're talking about hiring into your company, what might well allow you to continue to grow your business is hiring help on the home front. Childcare, cleaning, and cooking are all things you can hire for that will free up some of your time to continue working on your business. Some mompreneurs told us that their businesses would not be possible without paying for childcare.

Maybe you're a solo practitioner and your company isn't well suited to bringing on staff—or maybe you're not ready to share your business yet. But we'll bet that an extra set of hands around the house sure wouldn't hurt. If help in your company won't help you grow, consider getting some help at home.

Hiring allows you to acquire expertise you don't have

In addition to working on what you're good at, hiring also enables you to get what you don't have. Jo Saul had a love of books and a Ph.D. in English before she and her partner opened their first book store. What she didn't have was retail knowledge. Jo says, "I hired an experienced manager off the bat. I couldn't have done it otherwise."

When you're starting out, you may not know where you need help in your business. (Or you may not be able to afford to hire.) After years in business for herself, Anne-Sophie Falconer hired a website partner to "fill in the gaps" in her own skill and interest sets. In an effort to increase sales, she hired someone to develop her website in Year 4 of her business.

If you know the areas you're weak in—great. You're a step ahead of the game. It may take you a while to articulate where you need help. Once you've figured out what you're lacking, it will be that much easier to go out and find it.

Hiring sets you up for further growth

Contrary to what your kids may think, there is only so much you can do as a mom and business owner in a day. Hiring people into your company can set you up for further growth. Here's how one successful mompreneur explains it: "Having employees has allowed my company to grow. Sure, it takes time to train employees, but it allows me the freedom to do the things I should. It removes the mind clutter. It's important to think about the value of tasks versus the value of growth. You need a good product, but you need good management more. I've seen companies with great products go under."

Imagine removing the "mind clutter." We love this! It's tough to grow if you're the butcher, the baker, and the candlestick maker. Only with the right support in place will you be able to take your business to the next level.

Hiring gives you a break

Motherhood is an unrelenting grind. And business ownership is a marathon. Put 'em together and what do you have? One tired mommy. Hiring someone for your business is a great way to simply give you a break. It means that it's not all on you, all the time. Of course you're responsible for your employee's performance, but if you can outsource even *some* responsibility, you might preserve your own sanity.

Everyone needs to get to the doctor and the drugstore. If your business has you so tightly chained that you can't get to a personal appointment or spend time with your kids on the weekends, then maybe hiring some help will give you a bit of a break. Even if it's just a mental one.

Challenges
....

It takes time to train and manage staff

When you invite someone to join your company, you can't just plunk them in a corner and hit the spa. Yes—the idea of hiring is to give yourself more flexibility to do what you need to do, but you'll need to spend some time teaching your protege the ropes before you can enjoy your freedom. Indeed, the very idea of the time it takes to train staff is so off-putting for some that they avoid it. Training staff and managing staff are major time commitments, but the upside is living in a world where you can take a certain job off your plate, and that's pretty compelling.

When the mompreneurs at SavvyMom.ca brought on staff, they had to transition from managing their own time to managing others. They say, "Having staff has changed things. In some ways it doesn't save you time because you have to supervise and keep everyone happy. It's been surprising how much headspace ends up being devoted to managing people."

Managing people may not come naturally

Starting a business and managing staff are two very different skills. In fact, the qualities that attracted you to entrepreneurship—creativity, freedom, self-direction—are quite different from the qualities that will make you a good boss. As a boss you'll need to provide direction, have patience, and sometimes hand hold.

Just like reading a spreadsheet or riding a bike, managing people is a skill. And if you've never been a boss before, this is something that you're going to have to learn. Somewhere between Glinda the Good Witch of the North and the Wicked Witch of the West, you will have to learn to strike the right balance with your staff. Just remember, it's all for a good cause: the more you can hand off to someone else, the more freed up you'll be to pursue your true business interests or carpool the kids to gymnastics.

It can be hard to just say no to micromanaging

We don't think it's a coincidence that control freaks are attracted to entrepreneurship. After all, the whole point of working for yourself is to control your own life. Even though growth means that you need to hire people into your business, it shouldn't come as a surprise that mompreneurs sometimes have a hard time letting go. We manage our kids' schedules, pack lunches, shuttle them around, and run our businesses too. Who's to fault a girl for wanting to be in charge? As Trish Magwood puts it, "Having other people do things for me means accepting that not every detail is going to be how I want it." By all means, hire yourself some help. You probably can't grow on your own, so be ready to let go a little.

BUSINESS SUITS OR BLUE JEANS?

You'll want to hire people who share your vision. For example, we're not looking for straightlaced at Admiral Road. In our business, we want people to be casual, fun, and hard-working—like us. What do you want the vibe in your office to be? Like the message we've so often repeated, know what you're doing this for. It will make it much easier for you to articulate to other people.

It can be hard to find the time to get your systems organized, but it'll save you time and headaches down the road, and ultimately you'll need them to grow.

Epilogue

The secrets of success

We've thought a lot about the concept of success over the past eight years. Back in early 2002, when we were on the brink of throwing our hats into the mompreneur ring, there were definitely some sleepless nights. Not only were we stepping off the conventional path (what self-respecting MBA was going to open a baby blanket company?) and risking our long-term best friendship—but for the love of God, what if we weren't successful? Oh, the panic.

If you're thinking about starting your own business, you've probably always been an achiever of one kind or another. You probably did quite well in your pre-baby career. Throughout your life you've set your mind to something and just done it. You've been awarded, lauded, praised, and promoted. Your success has been clear for all the world to see. Jumping into the pool of mompreneurship will mean that your idea of success is about to be seriously challenged.

In this book, we have told you about mompreneurs who have been more financially successful than they ever imagined. But we also met many mompreneurs who are toiling away in their businesses and have yet to reach their financial goals. And then there are mompreneurs with truly heart-wrenching tales: businesses that went bust despite best efforts, partnerships that left former friendships in tatters, and even marriages that couldn't survive.

In light of the good, the bad, and the sticky, we asked each woman we were in touch with the following question: Are you successful? Overwhelmingly, the answer was the same: yes. Most of these women haven't won awards, haven't been featured on *Oprah*, and haven't seen a mad increase in sales. Yet, according to them, they are successful despite the fact that they work extremely hard and aren't necessarily bringing home the big bucks. What gives?

Early on in the life of Admiral Road, Danielle had an epiphany that cleared up this concept for us in a major way. Here is what happened, in her words: "When Amy and I were about to start Admiral Road I felt nearly sick with anxiety. One night, in a moment of fret, I asked my husband, Angus, 'What if I'm not successful at this?' He looked at me and said, 'Danielle, success is being happy.' Success. Is. Being. Happy. This quite literally rocked my world—it was a light bulb moment and it changed everything for me from that moment forward."

Mompreneurs know that life is not two-dimensional. It's not just about work *or* family; a career *or* staying at home with the kids; financial freedom *or* financial dependence. As moms—professional, ambitious, loving moms—the different parts of our lives mesh and blend and spill into each other. And like feeding a newborn, it can get very messy.

What mompreneurs also know is that there is more than one way to define success. When we asked what success meant to them, some of the mompreneurs said success was about making money. *These were fewer than ten percent of the nearly three hundred women we talked to.*

Rather, most of the mompreneurs seemed to share a more holistic vision of success. Lisa Will of Stonz says that she is successful by her own standards: "Success to me means personal flexibility, achieving goals, and having happy employees and strong products that people like and buy." Celebrity gifting guru Julie Kenney says that she's successful because "I go to bed and wake up loving what I do. It's not about the money, it's about doing what I love."

Erica Ehm echoes this sentiment: "I am more successful than my wildest dream. What don't I have? I've got it all. As a result of my business, my social network has exploded. That's a long way from the postpartum depression I had when my son was born. When starting your own business, the chance of making a lot of money is small. You do it because the process turns you on."

Another mompreneur says, "I'm successful because I just did it. I followed my dream. I made it happen." Some mompreneurs see themselves as successful by virtue of not having given up. Others find their success in simply having created something that is now out there in the world.

Others can find success in dictating their own schedule, even if they don't always love what they do. One mompreneur we met told us that she really doesn't love her business. According to her, "I don't enjoy my work. I wish I created something that made people happy or made a difference. I'm successful in that I do a good job for my clients and I know I'm a far better mom than I could be if I was working outside the home—and that makes me successful."

Still, she reflects, "It's a job. It's not all going to be rosy and happy—but if the payoff is clear then it can be worth it. On my worst possible day, the idea of going back to a fuzzy cubicle is still fathoms worse. I'd never have it any other way."

This comment really resonates with us. Part of the reason we wanted to write this book is to dispel the myth that mompreneurship is some kind of perfect life. As we like to say, "This is not your Barbie Dream Castle business!" Just like any job, there are ups and downs—things we enjoy and things we'd really rather not have to do. It's possible to love your job sometimes and just show up for work at other times. While we think it's ideal to love what you do and truly be passionate about it, we think that a mompreneur can also derive a lot of happiness simply by owning her schedule and controlling her future. Nearly all of the mompreneurs we've met truly love what they do—but even if they don't, they love the freedom and satisfaction that self-employment provides.

We love that the mompreneurs are positive, hopeful, and inspiring when it comes to their sense of success. Overwhelmingly, they give themselves top marks. Jacqui Meiers, mom of a five-year-old girl and owner of GoneShopping.ca, sums it up: "To some people success is a big job title. To some people it's earning a lot of money. I like to think of myself as successful. My work-life balance is blended well. My business is thriving and I'm learning and I've got my family. Success means you have to be happy. A happy mom means a happy kid and a happy husband."

Even those women who didn't find a pot of gold at the end of their journey call their experiences successful. As Quita Alfred put it, "Even if my business was not a financial success, the experience was very successful. It made me more interested in and determined to pursue a new venture. I love the process." Another mompreneur told us, "I've loved the experiences, the travel, trade shows, meeting people. This has been something else in my life—another identity. But I love being a mom too. Even if my business doesn't become a success, it's enriched my life in so many ways."

Women, and moms in particular, can be so hard on themselves. We question ourselves at every turn. We don't ever know if we're "doing it right." There are so many things to fail at, and the stakes—with our businesses, and especially our children—are so very high. Just like the experience of motherhood, your business is a work in progress. Some of the women we met were reflective regarding their definition of success. Andrea Page of FitMom puts it beautifully: "I'm more successful than I have ever been but not as successful as I can be. It's a journey, not a destination."

We couldn't agree more. As parents we've learned that we're not going to get everything right all the time, and we've come to understand that raising our business, like raising our kids, is a marathon and not a sprint. Robyn Green-Ruskin of Movies for Mommies says it perfectly: "Some days I'm Superwoman and some days I'm not doing anything well: I'm not a good wife, mom, or business-woman. It's a law of averages."

We're so gratified to have found a common thread among the mompreneurs: success is best viewed in the context of their whole lives.

As for us, well, we've got a few years under our belt now, both as parents and entrepreneurs. As the kids grow, their needs and what our families look like are changing. So too is our business. We're just about done with diapers, and we don't pack the blankets ourselves anymore. It's just an evolution. Is it easier? Yes. And no. It's different. As mothers and business owners we're calmer and more reflective than we used to be. We don't sweat the small stuff quite as much. We recognize when one of the kids is in "a phase" and we don't panic if we have a tough month at work. We have a clear sense of what we want our business to be. We've come to be able to answer the following questions: How big do we want to grow? What does our business stand for? Where does it fit in with the rest of our lives?

Our babies and our business have taught us so much. We're definitely smarter than we were a few years ago, but we know with certainty that we're not as smart as we will be a few years from now. The journey is truly what's worthwhile. And being on it together has made it all the more meaningful.

And it's true that while we're much less successful monetarily today than we would be had we stayed on the corporate career path, we have the incredible riches of balance and happiness that we feel sure would have eluded us had we stayed in our downtown jobs. Being available to our families while growing a terrific business has been the best path to success we could have imagined.

So what's your definition of success? Like anything else, it doesn't need to work for anyone else—it's all yours. Will you be successful when you make your first million? Great. Or will you be successful if you can volunteer in your child's class once a week? Also great.

Life as a mompreneur is good, bad, and sticky. Starting a business while raising children is at the same time daunting, thrilling, and enriching. The best thing you can have in your toolbox as you embark upon this exciting journey is a clear sense of what success means to you. However you define achievement and wherever your path takes you, we wish you the best.

Bon voyage.

Acknowledgements

We owe a huge debt of gratitude to many people who helped us get this project off the ground and supported us throughout.

For their advice early on, thanks to Luke Ballon, Amy Black, Ricky Englander, Diane Flacks, Doug Linton, Tanya Linton, Donna Shear, Brooke Shulman, and Emma Waverman.

Thank you to all of the inspiring mompreneurs who gave their time to be a part of this book. Whether you met us for coffee, talked to us on the phone, or completed our survey, we could not have written this book without your wisdom and advice. We hope you will feel that this book tells your story as much as it does ours.

We owe a decade of gratitude to Rebecca Reuber. Thank you not only for working on this project with us, but also for your mentorship and friendship over the years.

We are fortunate to have wonderful friends and family who read this book in early incarnations and provided invaluable feedback. An enormous thank you to Lawrence Ballon, Angus Botterell, Jill Briggs, Tanya and Lars Fenkell, Joanne Foster, Kate Hilton, Marci O'Connor, Madelaine Roig, Ian Schnoor and Carol Sherman.

Heartfelt thanks to Lizz Bryce. Thank you for not only contributing to the administration of this project, but for being a faithful friend to us and our families and for always making our lives easier by keeping Admiral Road running smoothly.

Thank you to the whole team at HarperCollins Canada—especially to Brad Wilson, our "Buddhist editor," for having more confidence in us than we had in ourselves. Thank you, Brad, for your patience with a couple of Type A Bay Street refugees.

This book would be nothing but an idea if not for Sara Angel, whose name could not be a more fitting descriptor. Thank you, Sara, for taking a cold call from a blanket company you'd once ordered from, and for dedicating countless hours of your time to helping us see this book through to completion. We are eternally grateful for your guidance, introductions, and thoughtful feedback, and we couldn't be happier about our new friendship.

Finally, thank you to our husbands, Angus Botterell and Ian Schnoor, for supporting this book project and our business in every possible way. Every success we have is due in no small part to your faith, love, and unending encouragement. If success is being happy, then there are no two more successful people around than us. Thank you, thank you, thank you.

Mompreneurs featured in this book

This is a listing of all of the mompreneurs we interviewed for this book, as well as a description of their businesses. Although not everyone was directly quoted, each woman we spoke to made a valuable contribution to the discussion and informed the direction of this book. Some of the quotes in the book came from sources not listed here, either because they were provided anonymously as part of our survey or because they were given casually outside the interview process.

Anita MacCallum
Mom to two girls, ages nine and six
Bookkeeper for a variety of small, owner-managed businesses.

Aqueous Limited
Paula Jubinville
Mom to an eight-year-old boy and seven-year-old girl
Paula Jubinville is a trusted business advisor and founder of Aqueous Limited.

The Baby and Toddler Shows Inc.
Melissa Arnott

Mom to two boys, ages nine and six

www.babytimeshows.ca

The Baby and Toddler Shows Inc. is the company behind The Ba-byTime Shows™, two consumer shows completely dedicated to pregnancy, birth, baby, and toddler.

Bee's Knees
Tammany Atkinson

Mom to two boys, ages eight and six

www.beeskneesbaby.com

Bee's Knees patented baby pants have neoprene padding in the knees to protect babies while crawling on hardwood and tile floors.

Betty and Bing Letterpress
Micheline Courtemanche

Mom to three girls, ages thirteen, ten, and seven

www.bettyandbing.com

Betty and Bing is a small letterpress studio situated in the pictur-esque town of Lunenburg, Nova Scotia.

BlueLoop
Jordan Maher

Mom to a six-year-old boy, three-year-old boy-and-girl twins, and a baby on the way

www.blueloop.ca

Social, educational, and parenting network for moms and moms to be.

Bugalug
Sundi Hoffman

Mom to two boys, ages seven and four

www.bugalug.ca

High-quality, innovative, and functional accessories for boys and girls, including a signature non-slip hair clip with a silicone grip.

Canadian Sitter Inc.
Martha Scully
Mom to two girls, ages eleven and eight
www.canadiannanny.ca
An online Canadian site designed to help families find nannies, babysitters, adult caregivers, pet care workers, and housekeepers. There are thousands of jobseekers to choose from.

Cleopatra Productions Inc.
Samantha Linton
Mom to three boys, ages thirteen, ten, and two
A production company specializing in high-quality erotica for women and couples.

DA Consulting
Debbi Arnold
Mom to two girls, ages seven and five
www.daconsult.ca
Debbi Arnold specializes in coaching entrepreneurs to create winning solutions for their business.

Debbie Bloomberg
Mom to a six-year-old girl
Criminal lawyer.

Diane Flacks
Mom to two boys, ages eight and three
www.dianeflacks.com
Writer and actor.

EchoAge

Debbie Zinman and Alison Smith

Debbie is mom to a nine-year-old boy and a six-year-old girl

Alison is mom to a nine-year-old boy and an eight-year-old girl

www.echoage.com

EchoAge is a charity-driven, eco-friendly, online birthday party service where children learn the value of giving and receiving while celebrating.

FitMom Inc.

Andrea Page

Mom to three boys, ages eleven, seven, and four

www.fitmomfitness.com

FitMom fitness programs are prenatal, postnatal, and beyond: yoga, personal training, and wellness for moms in the childbearing years and beyond. FitMom offers programming, training, consulting, and media products.

Gemini Consulting

Hyla Pollak (formerly with Discovery Toys)

Mom to three girls, ages seventeen, thirteen, and eleven, and a fifteen-year-old-boy

416.398.5335

Training for network marketing skills such as sales, and recruiting and team building. Gemini helps companies sell and market their product through network marketing.

GoneShopping.ca

Jacqui Meiers

Mom to a five-year-old girl

www.goneshopping.ca

Canadian lifestyle online store that offers stylish and practical products.

Harmony Fitness
Ali Lubin
Mom to three boys, ages seven, five, and two
www.harmonyfitness.ca
Harmony Fitness offers a unique fitness experience.

Honey-bunch.com
Nicole Morell
Mom to a seven-year-old girl and a four-year-old boy
www.honey-bunch.com
Online children's toy, gift, and party supply shop.

InQb8 Quilts
Quita Alfred
Mom to a six-year-old boy
416.878.9503
A small design studio producing baby quilts, custom order quilts, and wall hangings.

Jewels and Pinstripes
Julie Kenney
Mom to two boys, ages six and three
www.jewelsandpinstripes.com
Jewels and Pinstripes is celebrity gifting at its finest, specializing in creating one-of-a-kind gift bags for high-profile charity events and celebrity milestones.

Kathy Buckworth
Mom to two girls, ages eighteen and eleven, and two boys, ages sixteen and eight
www.kathybuckworth.com
Author, television personality, and public speaker.

Kid Brother Clothing
Carol Pitre
Mom to two boys, ages nine and seven, and a four-year-old girl
www.kidbrother.ca
Kid Brother is an urban line of clothing exclusively for boys with funky, practical clothes in high-quality fabrics and materials.

KidsAroundCanada (Kidding Around Communications)
Joanne Schneeweiss
Mom to two girls, ages eight and six
www.kidsaroundcanada.com
KidsAroundCanada.com is a national parenting website, keeping families "in the know" about valuable resources through an events calendar, e-magazine, directories, coupons, contests, and more.

Kids & Company Ltd.
Victoria Sopik
Mom to six boys, ages twenty-four, twenty-three, twenty, seventeen, fifteen, and thirteen, and two girls, ages twenty-one and eighteen
www.kidsandcompany.ca
Corporate childcare with guaranteed flexible care for children up to thirteen years old, with locations across Canada.

Kitsel, LLC
Samantha Rosenberg
Mom to a four-year-old boy
www.kitsel.com
Online baby gear store designed to take your ordinary baby to extraordinary, allowing him or her to express themselves through cool baby and toddler clothing.

Kriss Communications Inc.
Naomi Kriss
Mom to three boys, ages seven, five, and one
www.krisscommunications.com
Kriss Communications helps architects and architecturally related businesses get better recognition for their work.

Lifeline Personal Training
Jennifer Salter
Mom to three boys, ages seven, six, and four
www.lifelinepersonaltraining.com
Personal trainer.

Lumiere Kids Inc.
Anne-Sophie Falconer
Mom to two girls, ages thirteen and eleven
www.lumierekids.ca
A manufacturer of whimsical children's accessories.

Mabel's Labels
Tricia Mumby
Mom to a five-year-old girl
www.mabel.ca
Labels for the stuff kids lose.

Magazine Network
Jan Frolic
Mom to two boys, ages eight and six, and a two-year-old girl
www.magnetwork.com
Media sales.

Mally Designs Ltd.
Nicole Garza
Mom to an eight-year-old boy and a six-year-old girl
www.mallybibs.com
Designer, manufacturer, wholesaler, and retailer of Mally Bibs, the original leather baby bib, and other useful and fun Canadian-made leather accessories, including leather change purses, bookmarks, passport holders, and art cards.

Mandy Webster Design
Mandy Webster
Mom to three boys, ages twelve, ten, and five
www.mandywebster.com
Mandy Webster Design is a one-stop shop combining graphic design and copywriting to create compelling concepts that capture the personality of your business.

Mannerisms
Roz Heintzman
Mom to a twelve-year-old girl and a nine-year-old boy
www.mannerisms.ca
Mannerisms is a fun game to teach kids manners and etiquette.

The Mogul Mom
Heather Allard
Mom to two girls, ages ten and seven, and a four-year-old boy
www.themogulmom.com
The Mogul Mom is for moms running a business and raising a family—and rocking both.

The Mom Entrepreneur
Traci Bisson
Mom to two boys, ages ten and six

www.themomentrepreneur.com
The Mom Entrepreneur offers tips, advice, and resources for balancing motherhood and running a company.

Movies for Mommies (Sunflower Productions Inc.)
Robyn Green-Ruskin
Mom to two boys, ages four and one
www.moviesformommies.com
Movies for Mommies is an event for moms to enjoy a grown-up movie in a baby-friendly cinema. Sunflower Productions Inc. is an event-planning and consulting company dedicated to meeting the needs of corporations, media, and businesses of all sizes that seek to connect their brands with niche markets and the public through meaningful events and creative marketing.

My Bump Maternity
Cheryl Atkinson
Mom to two girls, ages eight and six, and a four-year-old boy
www.mybumpmaternity.com
My Bump is Toronto's destination for maternity fashions and breastfeeding needs that help you look and feel your best. Be proud and show off your bump!

MyGloss.com/GLOSS Inc. (Former owner of Modernmom.com)
Lolita Carrico
Mom to two boys, ages nine and six
www.mygloss.com and www.lolitacarrico.com
A multi-media brand delivering high-quality and high-interest women's content, videos, and community.

Name Your Tune Inc.
Candace Alper
Mom to a seven-year-old girl

www.nameyourtune.com
A children's music CD compilation that is made to order and personalized for each child. Children will hear their name more than eighty times throughout fourteen much-loved songs.

Nummies Lingerie
Alison Kramer
Mom to two boys, ages eight and six, and a four-year-old girl
www.nummies.com
A Canadian company making beautiful bras for nursing moms and moms-to-be.

Pippalily and Simply on Board
Victoria Turner
Mom to two girls, ages five and one, and a three-year-old boy
www.pippalily.com and www.simplyonboard.com
Pippalily creates practical parenting tools, with style. Simply on Board creates toy straps to keep baby's favourites off the ground.

Red Thread Design
Devorah Miller
Mom to three girls, ages ten, seven, and five
www.redthreaddesign.ca
Red Thread is a Canadian-made line of children's clothing known for its versatility and its bold use of prints and colour. Devorah designs and produces the line locally and ethically in her home city of Toronto.

rock-it promotions, inc.
Debra Goldblatt
Mom to a one-year-old girl
www.rockitpromo.com

A full-service public relations firm that specializes in lifestyle, health, hospitality, and much more.

Sacha Hayward
Mom to two boys, ages five and three
Harvey Kalles Real Estate Ltd.
www.harveykalles.com
Real estate agent.

Salsa Babies Inc.
Jennifer Torres
Mom to two girls, ages nine and six
www.salsababies.com
Dance classes for new moms and their babies. Salsa Babies also offers classes for toddlers and older kids as well.

SavvyMom Media
Sarah Morgenstern and Minnow Hamilton
Sarah is mom to two girls, ages nine and six, and an eight-year-old boy
Minnow is mom to two boys, ages thirteen and eleven
www.savvymom.ca
Online publisher of practical solutions for Canadian moms' everyday dilemmas delivered through a suite of email newsletters and websites: SavvyMom Today, ShareSavvy, EatSavvy, Shop Savvy, and more.

Stacey Helpert
Mom to two boys, ages eight and six, and a two-year-old girl
www.staceyhelpert.ca
Event planner.

Stonz
Lisa Will
Mom to a seven-year-old boy and a five-year-old girl

www.stonzwear.com
Stonz makes innovative, functional, and stylish outdoor kids gear.

Style Kid
Alison Lim
Mom to a nine-year-old boy and a five-year-old girl
www.stylekid.com
A Canadian online retailer of everything for babies and kids.

Summer Fun Guide
Elisa Palter (former owner of Help! We've Got Kids)
Mom to two girls, ages seventeen and thirteen, and one sixteen-year-old boy
www.SummerFunGuide.ca
The Ontario Summer Fun Guide is a comprehensive online directory of events, attractions, and outdoor activities in Ontario.

SupperWorks
Joni Lien and Chris Wood
Joni is mom to two girls, ages nineteen and sixteen
Chris is mom to a seventeen-year-old girl and a fifteen-year-old boy
www.supperworks.com
SupperWorks is a meal assembly business. SupperWorks creates the recipes, and does the shopping, washing, chopping, and clean-up so customers can prepare delicious, wholesome meals without the time, without the hassle, and without the mess!

Sweetpea Baby Food and Organic Snacks
Tamar Wagman and Eryn Green
Tamar is mom to a six-year-old boy and a three-year-old girl
Eryn is mom to a one-year-old girl
www.sweetpeababyfood.com

Manufacturers of frozen, organic baby food and organic toddler cookies sold through grocery and health food stores nationally.

Trish Magwood
Mom to one boy, age seven, and two girls, ages five and two
www.trishmagwood.ca
Founder of dish cooking studio, chef, TV personality, and author of two cookbooks.

Two Rooms (no longer in operation)
Elizabeth Kaiden
Mom to two boys, age ten and four, and one girl, age nine
Two Rooms offered childcare and workspace to parents working freelance or from home while caring for their young children.

TYPE Books
Jo Saul
Mom to an eight-year-old girl and a three-year-old boy
www.typebooks.ca
TYPE books is an independent bookstore with two locations in Toronto.

WeeHands
Sara Bingham
Mom to a ten-year-old boy and an eight-year-old girl
www.weehands.com
WeeHands is the world's leading children's sign language and language development program for babies, toddlers, and preschool children. WeeHands produces and distributes sign language products and classes for babies, toddlers, and preschool children.

Wrightway Premium Incentives/L'il Apples
Michelle Wright
Mom to an eight-year-old girl and a six-year-old boy
www.wrightwaypremiums.com and www.lil-apples.com
Manufacturer of children's hooded poncho towels.

Yummy Mummy Club
Erica Ehm
Mom to a ten-year-old boy and a seven-year-old girl
www.yummymummyclub.ca
Yummy Mummy Club speaks to the woman in every mom and is the online destination for modern mothers looking for guilt-free adult stimulation.

Index